The Fisher Model and Financial Markets

The Fisher Model

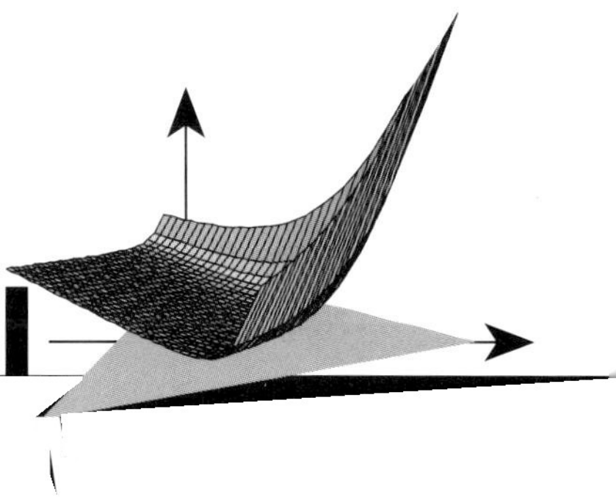

Richard D. MacMinn

Illinois State University, USA

World Scientific

NEW JERSEY • LONDON • SINGAPORE • BEIJING • SHANGHAI • HONG KONG • TAIPEI • CHENNAI

Published by

World Scientific Publishing Co. Pte. Ltd.

5 Toh Tuck Link, Singapore 596224

USA office: 27 Warren Street, Suite 401-402, Hackensack, NJ 07601

UK office: 57 Shelton Street, Covent Garden, London WC2H 9HE

Library of Congress Cataloging-in-Publication Data
MacMinn, Richard D.
The Fisher model and financial markets / by Richard D. MacMinn.
p. cm.
Includes bibliographical references and index.
ISBN 981-256-407-1 (alk. paper)
1. Corporations--Finance--Mathematical models. 2. Finance--Mathematical models. I. Title.

HG4012.M33 2005
332'.01'5118--dc22

2005050603

British Library Cataloguing-in-Publication Data
A catalogue record for this book is available from the British Library.

Typeset by Stallion Press
Email: enquiries@stallionpress.com

Printed by FuIsland Offset Printing (S) Pte Ltd, Singapore

Dedication

This monograph grew out of a lecture on the Fisher Model and Financial Markets that I wrote in July of 1984. I subsequently presented it and other lectures included here in my Ph.D. course on Uncertainty in Economics and Finance from 1984 till 2000. My Ph.D. students were a source of inspiration and insight. I valued them then as students and value them now as colleagues and friends. I dedicate this monograph to them.

Contents

Preface

This monograph represents work begun in July of 1984. Like a number of economists making the transition to finance, I wanted to gain some perspective on and appreciation for the finance discipline and, like others, I did not find a coherent perspective anywhere in the literature. While the Fisher model (1930) had been used in a number of corporate finance texts to note the foundations of the net present value rule, e.g., Brealey and Myers (1991), it had not been developed further in textbooks as a perspective for students of the finance discipline.[1] This work represents an attempt to articulate corporate finance from a common perspective and model. By generalizing the Fisher model to include risks, it is possible to exposit and prove the classic corporate finance theorems and to establish a common foundation for the discipline. For me it has been much like my first real analysis course that provided the first opportunity to really learn the calculus. Here the classic theorems of corporate finance are collected, stated, and some are proved. The reader is challenged to prove corollaries and theorems and to see how the model provides the fundamental building blocks for the discipline.

The Fisher model is summarized in Chapter 1 and subsequently generalized along the lines first used by Arrow and Debreu, i.e., see Arrow (1963) and Debreu (1959). A simple two-date Fisher model is constructed in a framework with all risk-averse agents and risks. The risks are the contracts exchanged *now* and paid *then*. The risk-averse agents exchange the risks and

[1] The Martin, Cox, and MacMinn text, i.e., Martin, J. D. *et al.* (1988). *The Theory of Finance: Evidence and Applications*. Dryden Press., subsequently provided more on the Fisher model than other texts but the Fisher perspective was not maintained, as I would have preferred.

behave in a self-interested manner to maximize expected utility subject to any relevant constraints. Introducing stocks to allow the transfer of money from *now* to *then* increases the dimension of the problem but otherwise leaves the standard constrained maximization problem, so common in standard microeconomic theory, in place. The simple stock contracts introduced by Arrow are easily seen to form the basis for the financial markets;[2] other securities such as corporate stocks and bonds are also introduced and valued as portfolios of the Arrow securities.

The standard economic assumption that risk averse agents behave in a self-interested manner is examined in Chapter 4. The classic Fisher separation result is that the agent selects the scale of an investment project independent of any preferences for consumption *now* versus *then* and the result follows from the notion that more is preferred to less, i.e., self-interested behavior. The investment scale selected by the agent is also the scale that maximizes net present value and so the classic Fisher separation result provides the foundation for that rule. The Fisher model has been extended here to include risks and risk-averse agents and so it is natural to consider how the self-interested proprietor or chief executive officer will behave. After specifying the compensation scheme, the chief executive officer has a decision problem that involves the selection of a portfolio of securities on personal account and an investment decision and financing decision on corporate account. A separation result flows from this analysis in much the same way that the classic Fisher separation result did. Similarly, the corporate objective function or equivalently the rule used by the manager in making decisions on corporate account also follows as a simple corollary. For some compensation schemes the corporate objective function is the maximization of current shareholder value subject to relevant constraints; hence, the analysis provides the foundation for the corporate objective function. What is more, it shows the connection between current shareholder value and net present value. The analysis also shows that the corporate objective function that is derived from this kind of analysis is not always current shareholder value. The compensation scheme will determine the objective function used by the manager and if the manager is compensated with stock options then the objective function becomes the maximization of the value of the stock option package. The maximization of stock option value can result in the acquisition of too much risk by the manager.

[2]The Arrow securities payoff one currency unit in a particular state and zero otherwise. Hence, the securities are unit vectors in the space of financial payoffs. The securities form a basis, i.e., minimal spanning set, for the financial markets. The Arrow securities are called basis stock here because of the analogy to linear algebra.

More contracts and values are introduced in Chapter 5 to provide a slightly different interpretation of debt and equity and to provide the contracts necessary in some of the subsequent analysis.

The classic theorems in corporate finance are introduced and some are proved in Chapter 6. The early theorems of Modigliani and Miller are proved using a few different methods and discussed in some detail because they are important to topics in subsequent chapters, e.g., the 1958 Modigliani–Miller Theorem has implications for corporate control and for risk management. Other theorems are stated but proved in subsequent chapters.

Agency problems similar to those discussed by Jensen and Meckling (1976) are introduced and discussed in Chapter 7. The classic principal-agent problem due to Ross (1973) is discussed here and reframed in a financial market setting as an agency problem. The agency problem is often due to a hidden action problem that will be discussed. The risk-shifting problem and the under-investment problem are both examples of the hidden action problem and a contracting solution is provided here for the risk shifting problem.

An agency problem may occur due to either a hidden action or a hidden knowledge problem. The hidden knowledge problem is considered in Chapter 8. One of the most well known implications of the hidden knowledge problem is found in Myers and Majluf's pecking order theorem. The pecking order theorem is demonstrated.

The notion of risk management is considered in Chapter 9. The corporation has long been viewed as a nexus of contracts in corporate finance and that perspective has generated a lot of insight. Even the organization of the discipline reflects this view. Capital structure theorems are concerned with a set of contracts. The selection of a capital structure for the firm is a risk management decision. Questions surrounding mergers and acquisitions are also concerned with contract sets; the decision to acquire or divest assets is an example of a risk management decision. Similarly, the decision to hedge currency, commodity, or interest rate risk is also a risk management decision. The chapter on risk management might be viewed as a logical extension of this nexus of contracts conception of the corporation. Within this framework, a hedging theorem due to Froot *et al.* (1993) is stated and proved.

Chapter 1

The Fisher Model with Certainty

The model introduced here was originally described by Fisher (1930) under conditions of perfect foresight. It is summarized here in preparation for the subsequent chapters on uncertainty.[1] This model provides three results that form the foundations for the theory of corporate finance. The model shows how one may develop the notion of the time value of money or the interest rate in a financial market model, how one may separate the savings decisions of individuals from the investment decisions of firms, and finally why the net present value rule is appropriate for decision making. All of these results flow from the Fisher model and so make it of central importance in the development of corporate finance. The certainty version of the model does not explain the existence of different rates of return on securities or other matters of concern but an uncertainty version of the model might be expected to provide insights and is developed in subsequent chapters; those chapters are all founded on what is developed here. Some remarks are included at the end of this chapter to outline what may be expected from a more general Fisher model.

Financial markets perform the role of allowing individuals and corporations to transfer money between dates. The individual may save by transferring dollars from the present to the future. The corporation may invest and finance the investment by transferring dollars from the future to the present. The following model provides the theoretical foundation for the net

[1]Those familiar with the Fisher model should proceed to the next chapter.

present value rule and by extension the corporate objective function. It also demonstrates why we look to the financial markets to find the cost of capital.

In its simplest setting, this model of individual behavior incorporates only one time period and does not include uncertainty. The model is developed in three steps. First, allowing the consumer to participate in the financial market, the individual's savings decision is characterized.[2] Second, the investment frontier is introduced and consumer is given the role of firm proprietor; although the net present value rule has not been derived yet, we assume that the proprietor makes an investment decision on behalf of the firm using that rule. This investment decision is in capital goods rather than financial assets. Third, the individual's savings decision is restored and the individual is given two roles. One role is firm proprietor and the other is consumer. The individual makes both decisions to maximize expected utility subject to the appropriate constraints. It should be noted that no objective function for the firm such as net present value is assumed here. Allowing the individual to make an investment decision as firm proprietor and to make a savings decision in the financial market as a consumer, the individual's savings and investment decisions are characterized. In the first and third steps, the individual is assumed to behave in accordance with her own self-interest. It is important to note that we are not assuming that the individual makes any decisions to maximize net present value. If any model is to demonstrate the importance of the net present value rule, then that model must show that the individual finds it optimal to use the rule. This result is demonstrated in case three.

Savings Decisions

Suppose the consumer stands at date zero and makes choices that will allocate income and consumption across two dates $t = 0$ and 1, that we refer to as *now* and *then* respectively. The consumer is endowed with some income *now* and *then*. Let $m = (m_0, m_1)$ denote the income pair, similarly let $c = (c_0, c_1)$ denote the consumption pair; each pair represents dollars *now* and *then*. Suppose the consumer can borrow and lend at the known interest rate r. Then the consumer selecting a consumption pair also makes a savings decision $s_0 = m_0 - c_0$; the savings choice yields $(m_0 - c_0)(1 + r)$ dollars *then*. The consumer must make these consumption choices consistent with a budget constraint

$$c_0 + \frac{c_1}{1+r} = m_0 + \frac{m_1}{1+r} \tag{1.1}$$

[2]Since there is no uncertainty, all financial assets must yield the same rate of return. Hence it is logical to suppose that there is only one financial asset and market. This will change when uncertainty is introduced.

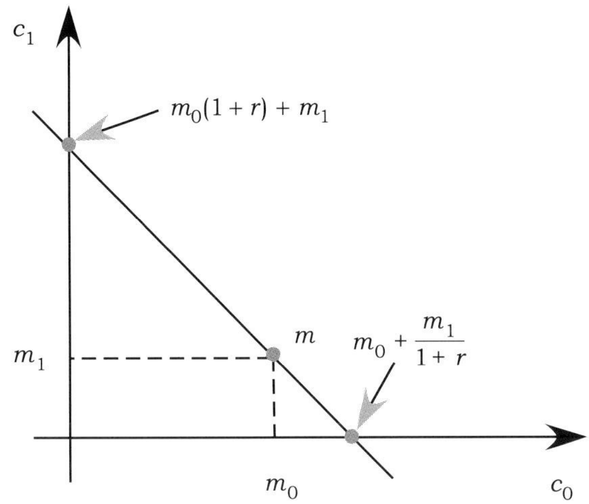

Figure 1.1 The budget constraint.

The budget constraint represents all the consumption pairs that equate the present value of the consumption plan with that of the income stream. The point $m = (m_0, m_1)$ in Figure 1.1 represents the time pattern of the income. Note that $(1 + r)$ is the absolute value of the slope of the budget constraint and corresponds to the increase in consumption *then* from each dollar saved *now*. A greater income either *now* or *then* yields a higher budget line through the new income pair. A greater interest rate yields a steeper budget line, since giving up a unit of consumption *now* would permit even more consumption *then*.

The consumer's preferences are represented by an intertemporal utility function $u(c_0, c_1)$. The utility maps consumption pairs into real numbers, i.e., the larger the number the better the consumption pair. The consumer is assumed to prefer more to less and so utility increases with more consumption *now* and *then*. The utility function also contains information concerning the consumer's preference for more consumption *now* versus *then* and this preference is consumer specific.

The preferences indicated by the utility function may be represented with intertemporal indifference curves; consumption pairs on an indifference curve, of course, indicate the same utility while the higher indifference curves represent greater utility. The absolute value of the slope of these curves at any consumption pair yields the individual's intertemporal marginal rate of substitution, i.e., *mrs*, and measures the value of consumption *now* in terms of consumption *then*. A steeper indifference curve corresponds to greater

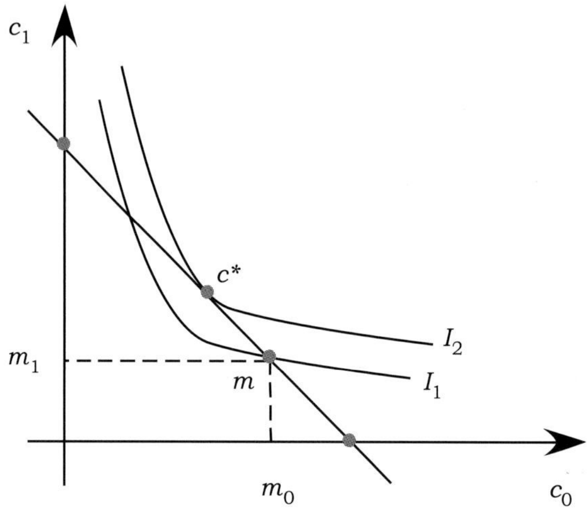

Figure 1.2 The optimal consumption.

desire for consumption *now*. The indifference curves in Figure 1.2 also illustrate the notion of a decreasing marginal rate of substitution, i.e., as the individual increases consumption *now*, the value of consumption *now* in terms of consumption *then* decreases.

The individual's choice problem may be characterized as a constrained maximization problem. The consumer selects the consumption pair to

$$\begin{aligned} &\text{maximize } u(c_0, c_1) \\ &\text{subject to } c_0 + \frac{c_1}{1+r} = m_0 + \frac{m_1}{1+r} \end{aligned} \tag{1.2}$$

The Lagrange function for this problem is

$$L(c_0, c_1, \lambda) = u(c_0, c_1) - \lambda\left(c_0 + \frac{c_1}{1+r} - m_0 - \frac{m_1}{1+r}\right) \tag{1.3}$$

The first order conditions for a maximum are

$$\frac{\partial L}{\partial c_0} = \frac{\partial u}{\partial c_0} - \lambda = 0 \tag{1.4}$$

$$\frac{\partial L}{\partial c_1} = \frac{\partial u}{\partial c_1} - \lambda\frac{1}{1+r} = 0 \tag{1.5}$$

$$\frac{\partial L}{\partial \lambda} = m_0 + \frac{m_1}{1+r} - c_0 - \frac{c_1}{1+r} = 0 \tag{1.6}$$

The solution to this problem is demonstrated in Figure 1.2. The marginal rate of substitution is the ratio of the marginal utility of consumption *now* to the

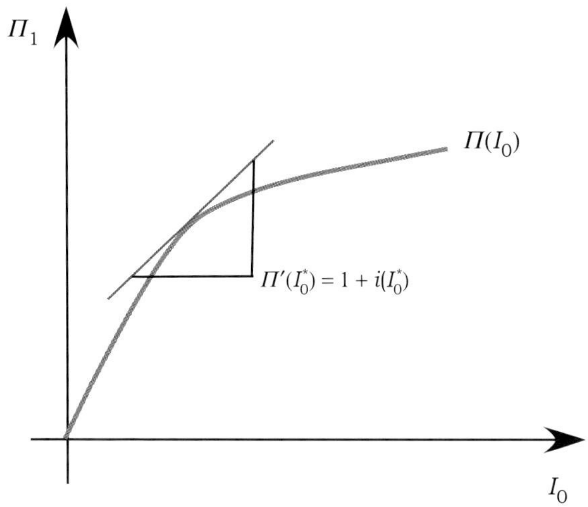

Figure 1.3 The investment frontier.

marginal utility of consumption *then*. From (1.4) and (1.5) it follows that

$$mrs = \frac{\frac{\partial u}{\partial c_0}}{\frac{\partial u}{\partial c_1}} = \frac{\lambda}{\lambda \frac{1}{1+r}} = 1 + r \tag{1.7}$$

Note that at the consumption bundle c^*, the consumer's marginal rate of substitution equals one plus the rate of interest, i.e., $mrs^* = 1 + r$. The optimality condition has a simple interpretation; it says that at the margin c^* the individual values consumption *now* in terms of consumption *then* at its opportunity cost.

The Investment Frontier

Next suppose the time pattern of income may be altered by investing in capital goods. Let I_0 denote the dollar investment in capital goods and Π_1 denote the total dollar return on the investment; let $\Pi_1 = \Pi(I_0)$ and suppose $\Pi(I_0)$, i.e., the investment frontier, is a function which increases at a decreasing rate in the dollar investment. The function Π is shown in Figure 1.3. The slope of the investment frontier at a point is $\Pi'(I_0) \equiv 1 + i(I_0)$, where i is an interest rate called the marginal efficiency of investment. Since the payoff Π_1 increases at a decreasing rate, the marginal efficiency of investment also decreases as I_0 increases.

The net present value and internal rate of return

Although the firm proprietor is not necessarily concerned with the net present value, or equivalently, the net future value, of the investment project, it is appropriate at this point to identify the investment level which maximizes the net present value. Let *npv* and *nfv* denote net present and future value, respectively. Then

$$npv(I_0) = -I_0 + \frac{\Pi(I_0)}{1+r} \tag{1.8}$$

and

$$\begin{aligned} nfv(I_0) &\equiv (1+r)npv(I_0) \\ &= -(1+r)I_0 + \Pi(I_0) \end{aligned} \tag{1.9}$$

Maximizing *npv* and *nfv*, of course, yields the same investment level. The derivative of net future value with respect to the investment level is

$$\begin{aligned} \frac{dnfv}{dI_0} &= -(1+r) + \Pi'(I_0) \\ &= -(1+r) + (1+i(I_0)) \\ &= 0 \end{aligned} \tag{1.10}$$

At the investment level which maximizes *nfv*, this derivative is zero and so the interest rate in the financial market equals the marginal efficiency of investment, i.e., $r = i(I_0^*)$. This condition simply says that the last dollar invested must yield the same rate of return as is available in the financial market. The investment I_0^* is shown in Figure 1.4. Note that the vertical distance between $\Pi(I_0)$ and $(1+r)\, I_0$ is the net future value and I_0^* maximizes this distance.

It is also possible to provide a graphical interpretation of the internal rate of return, i.e., *IRR*, on the project. The internal rate of return is implicitly defined as that rate of return which yields a zero net present value, or equivalently, a zero net future value. Hence, the $IRR(I_0)$ is implicitly defined by the condition

$$nfv(I_0) = -\,(1 + IRR(I_0))\, I_0 + \Pi(I_0) = 0 \tag{1.11}$$

or equivalently, by the condition

$$1 + IRR(I_0) = \frac{\Pi(I_0)}{I_0} \tag{1.12}$$

This shows that one plus the internal rate of return can be interpreted graphically as the slope of a cord from the origin to a point on the investment

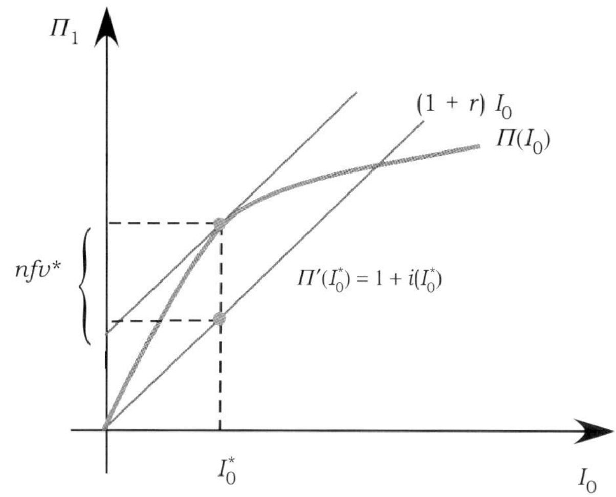

Figure 1.4 The investment that maximizes *npv* and *nfv*.

frontier. Note that if, as assumed, $\Pi(I_0)$ increases at a decreasing rate then the internal rate of return decreases in I_0.

The Optimal Investment and Savings Decisions

Finally, suppose the individual not only selects a consumption plan but also an investment plan in capital goods. The consumer then effectively becomes a single proprietor. The ability to invest in capital goods alters the individual's income pair from (m_0, m_1) to $(m_0 - I_0, m_1 + \Pi(I_0))$. The constrained maximization problem becomes a choice not only of an optimal consumption plan c^* but also an optimal investment. Hence, the constrained maximization problem is

$$\begin{gathered}\text{maximize } u(c_0, c_1) \\ \text{subject to } c_0 + \frac{c_1}{1+r} = m_0 - I_0 + \frac{m_1 + \Pi(I_0)}{1+r}\end{gathered} \tag{1.13}$$

The budget constraint is simply the condition that the present value of consumption plan equals the present value of income stream. The position of the budget constraint is determined by the investment decision because that decision alters the income pair. The individual has two roles. One of the roles is as the proprietor of a firm. In that capacity the individual makes the investment decision. The other role is that of a consumer. In this capacity, the individual selects the pair (c_0, c_1), or equivalently, a savings level. The

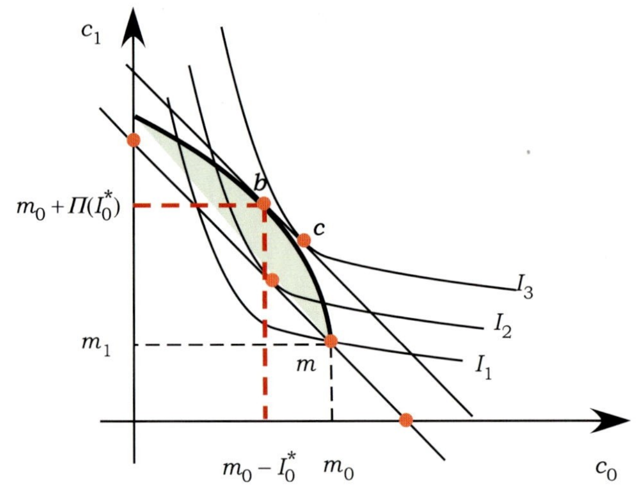

Figure 1.5 Fisher separation.

feasible investment and consumption decisions are represented by the investment frontier and the associated budget line, respectively, in Figure 1.5.

The Lagrange function for the constrained maximization problem in (1.13) is

$$L(c_0, c_1, I_0, \lambda) = u(c_0, c_1) - \lambda\left(c_0 + \frac{c_1}{1+r} - (m_0 - I_0) - \frac{m_1 + \Pi(I_0)}{1+r}\right) \tag{1.14}$$

The first order conditions are (1.4), (1.5), and

$$\frac{\partial L}{\partial I_0} = -\lambda\left(1 - \frac{\Pi'(I_0)}{1+r}\right) = 0 \tag{1.15}$$

$$\frac{\partial L}{\partial \lambda} = (m_0 - I_0) + \frac{m_1 + \Pi(I_0)}{1+r} - c_0 - \frac{c_1}{1+r} = 0 \tag{1.16}$$

Note that first order condition (1.15) yields $i(I_0^*) = r$ as the condition for an optimal investment; this is the familiar marginal efficiency of investment equal the interest rate common in other economic models. The individual, in the role of proprietor, selects the investment level indicated by the pair $(m_0 - I_0^*, m_1 + \Pi(I_0^*))$. Then, the individual, in the role of consumer, selects the consumption bundle indicated by the point c^*. Note that, at b

the condition $i(I_0^*) = r$ holds, while at c the condition $mrs = 1 + r$ holds. Also, observe that the condition $i(I_0^*) = r$ does not depend on the individual's preferences and that it is the condition for a maximum net present value.

An alternative intuitive explanation is as follows: The individual has preferences consistent with the observation that more is preferred to less. The individual selects the investment plan $(I_0^*, \Pi(I_0^*))$ which maximizes the present value of total income, because by doing so the individual obtains the highest possible budget line in the financial market. To see this, note that the budget line for any investment decision intersects the horizontal axis at

$$\begin{aligned} m_0 - I_0 + \frac{m_1 + \Pi(I_0)}{1+r} &= m_0 + \frac{m_1}{1+r} - I_0 + \frac{\Pi(I_0)}{1+r} \\ &= m_0 + \frac{m_1}{1+r} + npv(I_0) \qquad (1.17) \end{aligned}$$

and the budget line maximizes this value and so it yields the greatest capability for consumption *now* and *then*. This is the Fisher separation result, i.e., all individuals, irrespective of their preference for consumption *now* versus *then*, select the same investment plan. Maximizing the present value of income is equivalent to maximizing the net present value of the investment. Recall that the analysis was not begun with the objective of maximizing the net present value. The objective was to maximize the individual's utility subject to a budget constraint and this yielded the result that any individual makes the investment decision to maximize net present value. Hence, the roles of proprietor and consumer can be separated.

Remarks

The Fisher model is remarkably robust for such a simple construct. It provides for a determination of an interest rate, for a Fisher separation theorem and for a derivation of the net present value rule. It is possible to derive the supply of and demand for savings based on the model developed here and so it is possible to determine an equilibrium rate of interest; that has not been pursued here because the analysis focuses on the development of corporate finance theory. For this development, the separation theorem plays an important role because it shows that an individual making a savings decision on personal account and a capital investment decision on firm or proprietorship account will separate the two decisions, in the sense that the capital investment decision will be made without reference to intertemporal preferences for consumption *now* versus *then*. Equivalently, the separation theorem shows that the investment decision is driven by the more is preferred to less assumption but not intertemporal preferences because the financial market allows the individual to reallocate consumption across time by borrowing or lending. Finally, the model also provides a decision rule for the single proprietor and that rule is to make decisions that maximize net present value.

The certainty version of the Fisher model has its limitations. The certainty model cannot explain different rates of returns for securities. As one would expect, the introduction of uncertainty provides the basis for explaining different rates of return and much more. Portfolio Theory (Markowitz 1952), the Capital Asset Pricing Model (Sharpe 1964; Mossin 1966; Garman 1979), the Arbitrage Pricing Model (Garman 1979), etc., have all been developed to provide various explanations in corporate finance but none have the capability of integrating the results in one framework. The Fisher model does as the subsequent chapters show. Arrow's work on the allocation of risk (1963) provides the foundation for a generalized version of the Fisher model. The savings decision becomes a portfolio decision as is shown in the next chapter. The subsequent chapters provide a demonstration of some of the key results and insights in corporate finance reframed and motivated in the context of the Fisher model.

Suggested Problems

1. Suppose the individual has intertemporal preferences specified by $u(c_0, c_1) = \min\{c_0, c_1\}$. Sketch the indifferences curves and show the optimal consumption bundle.
2. Suppose the individual has the intertemporal preferences specified in the last problem and an income pair such that $m_0 > m_1$. Does the individual lend or borrow in the financial market? How does the lending or borrowing decision change given an increase in the interest rate?
3. Let the investment frontier be specified as $\Pi(I_0) = \min\{\kappa I_0, M\}$ where κ and M are positive constants. Sketch this frontier. Also provide a sketch of the marginal efficiency of investment and the internal rate of return.
4. Show that $nfv(I_0) > 0$ implies $IRR(I_0) > r$ and that $nfv(I_0) < 0$ implies $IRR(I_0) < r$.
5. Suppose $\Pi' > 0$ and $\Pi'' < 0$. Show that $i < IRR$ for all positive investment levels.
6. Provide a sketch of an investment frontier which would yield a negative net present value for any positive level of investment.
7. Why is it reasonable to say that the financial market rate of return r is the cost of capital?
8. Sketch the case in which any positive investment in a project yields a negative npv and show that the consumer\proprietor chooses not to invest.

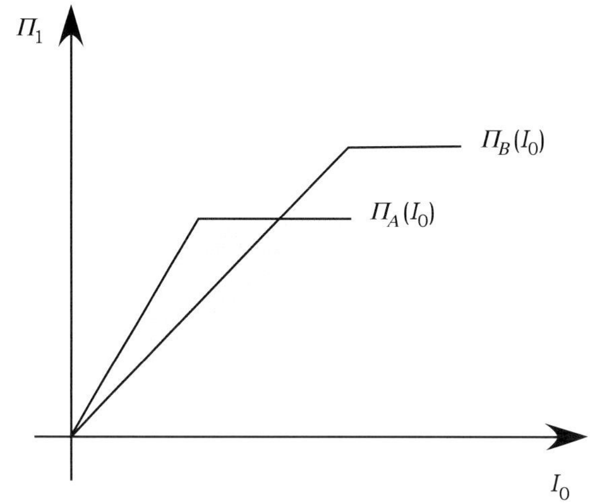

Figure 1.6 Mutually exclusive projects.

9. Show how the proprietor's investment choice is affected by a reduction in the interest rate r.
10. Suppose that the proprietor selects an investment level either greater than or less than the level b shown in Figure 1.5. Show that, in either case, the individual is worse off and that this result does not depend on whether the individual is a borrower or lender.
11. Suppose the proprietor can invest in one of two mutually exclusive projects. Let Π_A and Π_B denote the investment frontiers for the two projects, so that $\Pi_A(I_0)$ is the revenue generated *then* if project A is selected and $\Pi_B(I_0)$ if project B is selected. The investment frontiers are shown in Figure 1.6. Show and explain the following:
    a. The Fisher separation result holds in terms of which project is selected as well as the scale at which the project is operated.
    b. Specify the conditions under which project B will be selected over project A.
    c. Which project has the larger internal rate of return? If you select project A or B on the basis of which has the larger *IRR*, is your choice consistent with your analysis in (b)?

Chapter 2

The Fisher Model

The Fisher model has been noted as one of the foundations of corporate finance for decades. In its classic form, the Fisher model (1930) posits the existence of a financial market that allows individuals to transfer money between dates at a known rate of interest.[1] Let those dates be known as *now* and *then*. Individuals have preferences over consumption *now* versus *then* and may implement those choices by saving or dissaving or equivalently by lending or borrowing in the financial market. Each individual makes a consumption choice that reallocates that individual's income stream. The choice is made to maximize utility subject to a budget constraint that limits choices to those that make the present value of the consumption stream equal to that of the income stream. The model was developed for a certain rate of return in the financial market. Some attention has subsequently been focused on the savings decision under uncertainty, e.g., Sandmo (1970) and Kimball (1990). The focus here is somewhat different; the focus is on the most natural extension of the classic Fisher model to a financial market in which the individuals, whom we will subsequently also call consumers or investors, allocate their consumption through time by selecting from a variety of assets. The model developed here is the basic construct for all the subsequent developments.[2]

[1]This classic model is also typically extended to allow the individual to make an investment decision, i.e., an investment in physical as opposed to financial capital. The extension will be considered in a subsequent chapter.

[2]Also see Hirshleifer, J. (1965). "Investment Decision Under Uncertainty: Choice-Theoretic Approaches." *Quarterly Journal of Economics* 79(4): 509–536. Hirshleifer provided a comparison of the Capital Asset Pricing Model and the Fisher model and was one of the motivations for the current model that provides a more robust generalization of the Fisher model in a financial market setting.

Consider a competitive economy operating between the dates *now* and *then*. Consumer i selects a consumption pair (c_{i0}, c_{i1}) where c_{i0} denotes consumption *now* and c_{i1} denotes consumption *then*. Let (m_{i0}, m_{i1}) denote the consumer's income *now* and *then*. Let $u_i(c_{i0}, c_{i1})$ be the consumer's increasing concave utility function; u_i expresses the individual's preferences for consumption *now* versus *then*. To introduce uncertainty let $(\Xi, \mathcal{F}, \Psi_i)$ denote the probability space for consumer i, where Ξ is the set of states of nature, $\mathcal{F}$ is the event space, and Ψ_i is the probability measure. We will initially suppose that there are only a finite number of states of nature, i.e., $\Xi = \{\xi_1, \xi_2, \xi_3, \ldots, \xi_N\}$, and for graphical purposes we let $N = 2$; in this case, the event space $\mathcal{F}$ is the power set, i.e., the set of all subsets of Ξ. To make the uncertainty operational, suppose that the consumer can transfer dollars from *now* to *then* by purchasing one or more of N risky assets; each basis asset in a complete market model is a promise to pay one dollar if state of nature ξ occurs and zero otherwise. Let $p(\xi)$ be the price of an asset that yields one dollar in state ξ and zero otherwise.

Consumer and Investor Behavior

The consumer selects a consumption plan that specifies a consumption level *now* and a consumption level for each state of nature that may occur *then*. In its classic form, the problem is stated as a constrained maximization problem. Due to the uncertainty concerning consumption *then*, we maximize expected utility subject to a budget constraint. Therefore the problem may be stated as follows:

$$\begin{aligned} &\text{maximize} \int_{\Xi} u_i(c_{i0}, c_{i1}) d\Psi_i \\ &\text{subject to } c_{i0} + \sum_{\Xi} p(\xi) c_{i1}(\xi) = m_{i0} + \sum_{\Xi} p(\xi) m_{i1}(\xi) \end{aligned} \tag{2.1}$$

where the left hand side of the constraint is the risk adjusted present value of consumption and the right hand side is the risk adjusted present value of income. The budget constraint is shown in Figure 2.1.

Given the finite number of states of nature, the expected utility may also be expressed as follows:

$$\int_{\Xi} u_i(c_{i0}, c_{i1}) d\Psi_i = \sum_{\Xi} u_i(c_{i0}, c_{i1}(\xi)) \psi_i \tag{2.2}$$

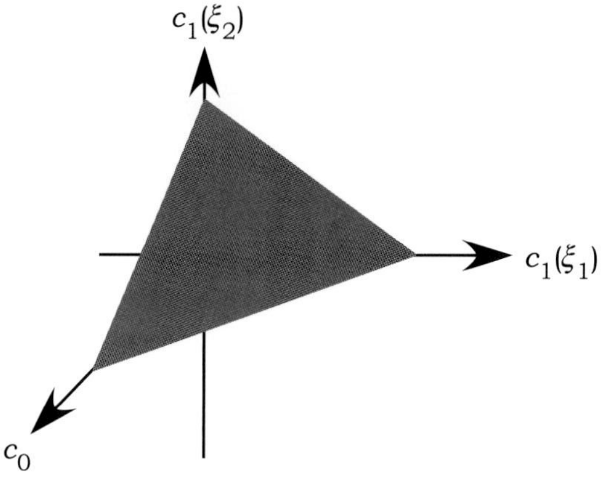

Figure 2.1 The budget constraint.

where $\psi_i(\xi)$ is the probability of state ξ. The problem may then be equivalently expressed as

$$\begin{aligned} &\text{maximize} \sum_{\Xi} u_i(c_{i0}, c_{i1}(\xi))\psi_i \\ &\text{subject to } c_{i0} + \sum_{\Xi} p(\xi)c_{i1}(\xi) = m_{i0} + \sum_{\Xi} p(\xi)m_{i1}(\xi) \end{aligned} \tag{2.3}$$

The first order conditions, for an optimal consumption number appropriately plan, are:

$$\sum_{\Xi} D_1 u_i \psi_i(\xi) - \lambda_i = 0^3 \tag{2.4}$$

$$D_2 u_i \psi_i(\zeta) - \lambda_i p(\zeta) = 0, \quad \text{for all } \zeta \in \Xi \tag{2.5}$$

Note that (2.4) simply says that the Lagrange multiplier λ_i equals the expected marginal utility of consumption *now*. Also observe that, using (2.4), (2.5) may be equivalently expressed as

$$p(\zeta) = \frac{D_2 u_i \psi_i(\zeta)}{\sum_{\Xi} D_1 u_i \psi_i(\xi)} \tag{2.6}$$

which says that the consumer will purchase state ζ claims up to the point at which its price equals the marginal rate of substitution, i.e., the rate at which

[3]The $D_1 u_i$ is notation for the partial derivative of the function u_i with respect to its first argument; similarly $D_2 u_i$ is the partial derivative with respect to the second argument.

the consumer is willing to sacrifice consumption *now* for more consumption in state ζ equals the price *now* of consumption in state ζ.[4]

It is also possible to consider the problem from the perspective of an investor. The investor selects a portfolio of securities to transfer dollars between dates and states. Let $x_i(\xi)$ be the number of state ξ shares purchased by investor i. Then the investor's problem may be rewritten in terms of the financial assets. Consumption *now* and *then* become

$$c_{i0} = m_{i0} - \sum_{\Xi} p(\xi)x_i(\xi) \tag{2.7}$$

and

$$c_{i1}(\xi) = m_{i1}(\xi) + x_i(\xi) \tag{2.8}$$

respectively. Now the investor's problem can be stated, in unconstrained form, as

$$\text{maximize} \sum_{\Xi} u_i\left(m_{i0} - \sum_{\Xi} p(\xi)x_i(\xi), m_{i1}(\xi) + x_i(\xi)\right)\psi_i(\xi) \tag{2.9}$$

where the consumption pair is expressed in terms of the financial assets. The first order conditions for the maximization problem are of the following form:

$$-p(\zeta)\sum_{\Xi} D_1u_i\psi_i(\xi) + D_2u_i\psi_i(\zeta) = 0, \quad \text{for all } \zeta \in \Xi \tag{2.10}$$

Note that these conditions may be restated as

$$p(\zeta) = \frac{D_2u_i\psi_i(\zeta)}{\sum_{\Xi} D_1u_i\psi_i(\xi)} \tag{2.11}$$

as previously in (2.6). Alternatively, we may note that

$$\frac{p(\xi_1)}{p(\xi_2)} = \frac{D_2u_i(c_{i0}, c_{i1}(\xi_1))}{D_2u_i(c_{i0}, c_{i1}(\xi_2))} \tag{2.12}$$

[4]Note that ζ is the Greek letter zeta. It and the Greek letter ω, i.e., omega, will be used throughout the analysis to denote particular states in Ξ. To see that the right hand side is the marginal rate of substitution, take the differential of the expected utility function, set it equal to zero, and note that this yields

$$\left(\sum_{\Xi} D_1u_i\psi_i(\xi)\right)dc_{i0} + (D_2u_i\psi_i(\xi))dc_{i1}(\xi) = 0$$
$$\Leftrightarrow -\frac{dc_{i0}}{dc_{i1}(\xi)} = \frac{D_2u_i\psi_i(\zeta)}{\sum_{\Xi} D_1u_i\psi_i(\xi)}$$

The right hand side of (2.12) is the investor's marginal rate of substitution while the left hand side is the price ratio. So this condition says that the investor selects state one and two claims such that the rate at which she is willing to sacrifice state two consumption for more state one consumption and remain indifferent equals that rate at which she can exchange state two claims for state one claims.

Having expressed the consumer's problem in a financial market setting, it is natural to consider the demand for the basis stock in this economy. These assets form the basis for the expression of all financial values. Since all other assets can be expressed in terms of a portfolio of the basis assets, those demands are perfectly elastic at the portfolio price or equivalently the arbitrage free price. The basis assets, however, may be expected to have downward sloping demand functions. The following section considers the development of the basis stock demand for a special case. The derivation of the demand and comparative statics in general case is left as an exercise.

Basis Stock Demand

Consider the demand for the basis stock. Let $x_i(\xi_j) \equiv x_{ij}$, $\psi_i(\xi_j) \equiv \psi_{ij}$ and $p(\xi_j) \equiv p_j$. Similarly, let $x_i = (x_{i1}, \ldots, x_{iN})$ denote the portfolio of basis stock, let $p = (p_1, \ldots, p_N)$ denote the vector of basis stock prices and let $\psi_i = (\psi_{i1}, \ldots, \psi_{iN})$ denote the vector of state probabilities. Now consider a special case of the utility function that eliminates the income effect. Let $u_i(c_{i0}, c_{i1}) = -\exp(-a_i[c_{i0} + c_{i1}])$ denote the utility function and let $H_i(x_i; p, \psi_i)$ denote the expected utility function, i.e.,[5]

$$H_i(x_i; p, \psi_i) = \sum_J u_i\left(m_{i0} - \sum_J p_j x_{ij}, x_{ij}\right)\psi_{ij} \tag{2.13}$$

The use of this utility function is motivated by Arrow's work. In a portfolio model with one safe asset and one risky asset, Arrow showed that non-increasing absolute risk aversion implies that the risky asset is a normal good.[6] Since the demand for any normal good is downward sloping and the

[5]This utility function yields a generalized form of the constant absolute risk aversion utility function. Note that

$$D_{11}u_i = -a_i D_1 u_i, \quad D_{22}u_i = -a_i D_2 u_i, \quad D_{12}u_i = -a_i D_2 u_i, \quad \text{and} \quad D_{12}u_i = -a_i D_2 u_i$$

This analysis must be generalized to allow for any utility function characterized by a generalized measure of decreasing absolute risk a version.

[6]See Arrow, K. J. (1974). "The Theory of Risk Aversion." *Essays in the Theory of Risk-Bearing*. North-Holland.

utility function assumed here satisfies a generalized notion of constant absolute risk aversion, it should follow that the demand functions are downward sloping. Given two states of nature, the first order conditions are

$$\begin{aligned} D_1H_i &= -p_1 \sum_J D_1u_i\psi_{ij} + D_2u_i\psi_{i1} = 0 \\ D_2H_i &= -p_2 \sum_J D_1u_i\psi_{ij} + D_2u_i\psi_{i2} = 0 \end{aligned} \tag{2.14}$$

It follows that the demand for basis stock one is a function $x_{i1}(p;\psi)$ and the slope of the demand function is

$$D_1x_{i1}(p;\psi) = -\frac{\begin{vmatrix} D_{13}H_i & D_{12}H_i \\ D_{23}H_i & D_{22}H_i \end{vmatrix}}{\begin{vmatrix} D_{11}H_i & D_{12}H_i \\ D_{21}H_i & D_{22}H_i \end{vmatrix}} \tag{2.15}$$

Since the second order conditions for a maximum are

$$D_{11}H_i < 0 \quad \text{and} \quad \begin{vmatrix} D_{11}H_i & D_{12}H_i \\ D_{21}H_i & D_{22}H_i \end{vmatrix} > 0 \tag{2.16}$$

the demand for basis stock one is downward sloping if the numerator is positive. Direct calculation yields $D_{23}H_i = a_ix_1$, $D_2H_i = 0$ and

$$\begin{aligned} D_{13}H_i &= -\sum_J D_1u_i\psi_{ij} + p_1x_{i1}\sum_J D_{11}u_i\psi_{ij} - D_{21}u_ix_{i1}\psi_{i1} \\ &= -\sum_J D_1u_i\psi_{ij} + a_ix_{i1}D_1H_i \\ &= -\sum_J D_1u_i\psi_{ij} \\ &< 0 \end{aligned} \tag{2.17}$$

since more is preferred to less, i.e., $D_1u_i > 0$. The sign of the determinant in the numerator of (2.15) is

$$\begin{vmatrix} D_{13}H_i & D_{12}H_i \\ D_{23}H_i & D_{22}H_i \end{vmatrix} = \begin{vmatrix} - & - \\ 0 & - \end{vmatrix} > 0 \tag{2.18}$$

It follows that the demand for basis stock one is downward sloping as shown in Figure 2.2.

Next, consider how the demand for basis stock one is affected by a change in the probability of state one. Note that in this two state example ψ_i can be treated as the probability of state one; then $1 - \psi_i$ is the probability of state

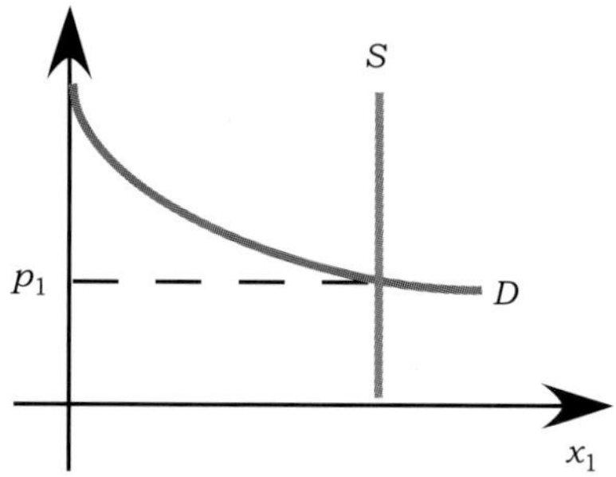

Figure 2.2 Basis stock demand.

two. The change in basis stock one demand, given a change in the probability of state one, is

$$D_3x_{i1}(p,\psi_i) = \frac{\partial x_{i1}}{\partial \psi_i} = -\frac{\begin{vmatrix} D_{15}H_i & D_{12}H_i \\ D_{25}H_i & D_{22}H_i \end{vmatrix}}{\begin{vmatrix} D_{11}H_i & D_{12}H_i \\ D_{21}H_i & D_{22}H_i \end{vmatrix}} \tag{2.19}$$

Direct calculation shows that $D_{15}H_i > 0$, $D_{25}H_i < 0$, and $D_{12}H_i < 0$. This derivative is positive if and only if the numerator is negative. The sign of the determinant in the numerator of (2.19) is

$$\begin{vmatrix} D_{15}H_i & D_{12}H_i \\ D_{25}H_i & D_{22}H_i \end{vmatrix} = \begin{vmatrix} + & - \\ - & - \end{vmatrix} < 0 \tag{2.20}$$

and so it follows that an increase in the probability of state one increases the demand for basis stock one, as expected. Other things being equal, this result implies an increase in the price of basis stock one. It may also be noted that there is a reduction in the demand for basis stock two since

$$D_3x_{i2}(p,\psi_i) = -\frac{\begin{vmatrix} D_{11}H_i & D_{15}H_i \\ D_{21}H_i & D_{25}H_i \end{vmatrix}}{\begin{vmatrix} D_{11}H_i & D_{12}H_i \\ D_{21}H_i & D_{22}H_i \end{vmatrix}} = -\frac{\begin{vmatrix} - & + \\ - & - \end{vmatrix}}{\begin{vmatrix} D_{11}H_i & D_{12}H_i \\ D_{21}H_i & D_{22}H_i \end{vmatrix}} < 0 \tag{2.21}$$

Other things being equal, this result implies a decrease in the price of basis stock two. Equivalently, *ceteris paribus*, the price ratio p_1/p_2 increases. Finally, it should be observed that the basis stock prices incorporate and aggregate the investors' preferences and probability beliefs. Any aggregate change in probability beliefs or risk preferences will result in a change in the composition of basis stock prices. A change in the risk preferences or probability beliefs of one investor will, of course, not change stock prices in this competitive market system.

Risk Aversion

Next consider risk aversion in this setting. It should be noted that the notion of risk aversion must be reframed in this setting since the notion of safe is different. How does the more risk averse investor behave? In a safe asset versus risky asset portfolio model, the more risk averse individual can be expected to purchase more of the safe asset, e.g., see Pratt (1964); Arrow (1984); MacMinn (1980); MacMinn (1984). In this model, what a more risk averse individual does in selecting a basis stock portfolio is an open question. By analogy, the more risk averse investor selects a basis stock portfolio which is safer, i.e., the more risk averse investor selects a basis stock portfolio closer to $c_1(\xi_1) = c_1(\xi_2)$. Suppose there are two investors i and k with the same probability beliefs, i.e., $\psi_i = \psi_k$ for all $\xi \in \Xi$. Recall that investor k is more risk averse than investor i if k has a utility function of the form $u_k = T(u_i)$, where T is an increasing concave function.[7] It is apparent that the first order conditions for investor k can be expressed as

$$p(\zeta) = \frac{D_2 u_k \psi_k(\zeta)}{\sum_\Xi D_1 u_k \psi_k(\xi)} = \frac{T' D_2 u_i \psi_i(\zeta)}{\sum_\Xi T' D_1 u_i \psi_i(\xi)} \tag{2.22}$$

and

$$\frac{p(\xi_1)}{p(\xi_2)} = \frac{D_2 u_k(c_{k0}, c_{k1}(\xi_1))}{D_2 u_k(c_{k0}, c_{k1}(\xi_2))} = \frac{T' D_2 u_i(c_{i0}, c_{i1}(\xi_1))}{T' D_2 u_i(c_{i0}, c_{i1}(\xi_2))} \tag{2.23}$$

Consider a comparison of the marginal rates of substitution. Due to the concavity of T,

$$\frac{T' D_2 u_i(c_{i0}, c_{i1}(\xi_1))}{T' D_2 u_i(c_{i0}, c_{i1}(\xi_2))} > \frac{D_2 u_i(c_{i0}, c_{i1}(\xi_1))}{D_2 u_i(c_{i0}, c_{i1}(\xi_2))} \tag{2.24}$$

if $c_{i1}(\xi_1) < c_{i1}(\xi_2)$. The inequality is reversed for $c_{i1}(\xi_1) > c_{i1}(\xi_2)$. Similarly, the marginal rates of substitution are equal when $c_{i1}(\xi_1) = c_{i1}(\xi_2)$. Other things being equal, this result suffices to show that the more risk averse individual selects a portfolio of basis stock that is safer. In Figure 2.3, investor

[7]See Mac Minn, R. (1984). Lecture Notes on Pratt's "Risk Aversion in the Small and in the Large" and its generalization. Pratt, J. W. (1964). "Risk Aversion in the Small and in the Large." *Econometrica* **32**: 122–136.

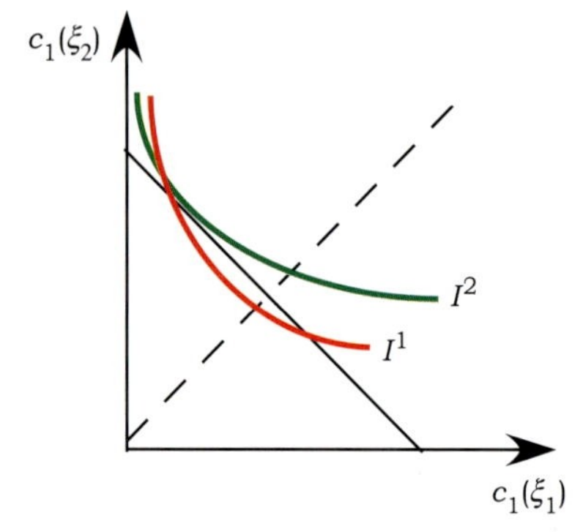

Figure 2.3 Risk aversion.

one is more risk averse than investor two. The I_1 and I_2 denote indifference curves in consumption *then* space. Note that at individual two's optimal consumption pair, we have the following relation

$$\text{mrs}_1 > \frac{p(\xi_1)}{p(\xi_2)} = \text{mrs}_2 \tag{2.25}$$

Since, from investor one's perspective, the value of stock one in terms of stock two exceeds the cost of stock one in terms of stock two, the more risk averse investor can increase expected utility by substituting type one for type two stock.

Remarks

We have seen in each statement of the problem that the individual will have an incentive to hold more than one type of asset or stock in spite of the fact that the prices differ.[8] This, of course, is due to risk aversion, i.e., the risk averse individual prefers a payoff in both states of nature to a payoff in only one even if the prices of the assets differ. Hence this model provides an explanation for the existence of different rates of return; recall that the rate of return on a basis stock that has a one dollar payoff in state ζ is

$$r(\zeta) = \frac{1}{p(\zeta)} - 1 \tag{2.26}$$

and so if $p(\zeta) > p(\xi)$ it follows that $r(\zeta) < r(\xi)$.

[8]It need not be true that $x_i(\xi) = 0$ for all $\xi \in \Xi$. However, even if $x_i(\xi) = 0$ it does not follow that the consumer is not selling shares in some corporation short because the corporations are simply portfolios of the stocks modeled here.

Suggested Problems

1. Suppose the investor's utility function takes the form $u(c_0, c_1(\xi)) = -e^{-a(c_0+c_1(\xi))}$ where a is a positive constant. Show that the constant a can be interpreted as a measure of absolute risk aversion. Will the investor hold the basis stock in fixed proportions independent of the measure of absolute risk aversion?
2. Suppose the investor's utility function takes the form $u(c_0, c_1(\xi)) = (c_0 + c_1(\xi))^{1-r}$, where r is a positive constant less than one. Show that r can be interpreted as a measure of relative risk aversion. Does this utility function provide a portfolio separation result?

Chapter 3

Financial Values

Having constructed the investor's portfolio problem, we are now in a position to value any security but will concentrate first on the corporation's equity, debt, and option issues. Each plays a role in determining the capital structure of the firm and each provides both explicit and implicit incentives for corporate decisions as we will see in subsequent chapters.

Equity

First consider the value of a firm's equity issue. Let $\Pi_f(\omega)$ denote the payoff *then* of corporation f. Suppose the corporation has previously issued N_f shares of common stock. If the firm is unlevered then the common stock payoff per share is Π_f/N_f. Now, allow each investor to select a portfolio of basis stock and the common stock of corporation f. The investor's consumption *now* and *then* are

$$c_{i0} = m_{i0} - \sum_{\Xi} p(\xi)x_i(\xi) - p_f x_{if} \tag{3.1}$$

$$c_{i1}(\xi) = m_{i1}(\xi) + x_i(\xi) + x_{if}\frac{\Pi_f(\xi)}{N_f} \tag{3.2}$$

where p_f is the share price and x_{if} is the number of shares of common stock f purchased by investor i. The first order conditions for the portfolio of basis stock are the same as equation (2.10) in Chapter 2. The first order condition for share of common stock f is

$$-p_f \sum_{\Xi} D_1 u_i \psi_i(\xi) + \sum_{\Xi} D_2 u_i \frac{\Pi_f(\xi)}{N_f}\psi_i(\xi) = 0 \tag{3.3}$$

Using equation (2.11), it follows that the share price may be expressed as

$$\begin{aligned} p_f &= \frac{\sum_{\Xi} D_2 u_i \frac{\Pi_f(\xi)}{N_f} \psi_i(\xi)}{\sum_{\Xi} D_1 u_i \psi_i(\xi)} \\ &= \sum_{\Xi} \frac{D_2 u_i \psi_i(\zeta)}{\sum_{\Xi} D_1 u_i \psi_i(\xi)} \frac{\Pi_f(\xi)}{N_f} \\ &= \sum_{\Xi} p(\xi) \frac{\Pi_f(\xi)}{N_f} \end{aligned} \tag{3.4}$$

Alternatively, the stock market value of this unlevered corporation is S_f, where

$$S_f \equiv p_f N_f = \sum_{\Xi} p(\xi) \Pi_f(\xi) \tag{3.5}$$

Hence, the stock market value of the corporation is the risk adjusted present value of its payoff, or equivalently, its quasi-rent.[1]

Debt

Next, consider the value of corporate bonds. Let a bond contract be a promise to pay one dollar in each state of nature. Then it should be clear that the price of the bond is p_b, where p_b is also a discount factor.

To reformulate the model to include debt, let p_b be the price of a safe bond contract and let y_i be the number of bond contracts purchased by investor i. The individual's consumption *now* and *then* become

$$c_{i0} = m_{i0} - \sum_{\Xi} p(\xi) x_i(\xi) - p_f x_{if} - p_b y_i \tag{3.6}$$

$$c_{i1}(\xi) = m_{i1}(\xi) + x_i(\xi) + x_{if} \frac{\Pi_f(\xi)}{N_f} + y_i \tag{3.7}$$

The first order conditions for the safe bond contract is

$$\sum_{\Xi} [-p_b D_1 u_i + D_2 u_i] \psi_i(\xi) = 0 \tag{3.8}$$

[1] The corporate payoff may be referred to as a quasi-rent in some cases because it does not include some or all of the capital expenses that would be part of a previous investment expenditure.

Using the first order conditions (3.8) and equation (2.11), note that this condition may be rewritten as

$$\begin{aligned} p_b &= \sum_{\Xi} \frac{D_2 u_i \psi_i(\zeta)}{\sum_{\Xi} D_1 u_i \psi_i(\xi)} \\ &= \sum_{\Xi} p(\xi) \end{aligned} \tag{3.9}$$

This is the expected result since the safe debt contract is equivalent to purchasing one share of stock of each type $\xi \in \Xi$. Any other result would yield an arbitrage opportunity. Let b_f be both the number of bond contracts and the promised payment on the bond issue. It follows that the value of a safe bond issue is $D_f(b_f) = p_b b_f$.

Next, consider risky debt instruments. Suppose firm f has issued bonds for which it promises to repay b_f dollars at the end of the period if the firm's earnings are sufficient. Then the return to all bondholders is $\min\{b_f, \Pi_f\}$. The return per share is $\min\{b_f, \Pi_f\}/b_f = \min\{1, \Pi_f/b_f\}$ and so letting p_{bf} denote the share price of the corporation's risky debt we have consumption *now* and *then* as

$$c_{i0} = m_{i0} - \sum_{\Xi} p(\xi) x_i(\xi) - p_f x_{if} - p_{bf} y_{if} \tag{3.10}$$

$$c_{i1}(\xi) = m_{i1}(\xi) + x_i(\xi) + x_{if} \max\left\{0, \frac{\Pi_f(\xi) - b_f}{N_f}\right\} + y_{if} \min\left\{1, \frac{\Pi_f(\xi)}{b_f}\right\} \tag{3.11}$$

The first order condition for debt purchase becomes

$$\sum_{\Xi} \left[-p_{bf} D_1 u_i + D_2 u_i \min\left\{1, \frac{\Pi_f}{b_f}\right\} \right] \psi_i(\xi) = 0 \tag{3.12}$$

Let $\min\{1, \Pi_f/b_f\} = 1$ for all states of nature in the subset $\Xi \backslash B$ and $\min\{1, \Pi_f/b_f\} = \Pi_f/b_f$ for all states of nature in the complement of $\Xi \backslash B$, i.e., B, then the first order condition (3.12) may be rewritten as

$$p_{bf} = \sum_{\Xi \backslash B} p(\xi) + \sum_{B} p(\xi) \frac{\Pi_f(\xi)}{b_f} \tag{3.13}$$

Notice that the total market value of the firm's risky debt is $D_f(b_f) = p_{bf} b_f$, or equivalently,

$$\begin{aligned} D_f &= \sum_{\Xi \backslash B} p(\xi) b_f + \sum_{B} p(\xi) \Pi_f(\xi) \\ &= \sum_{\Xi} p(\xi) \min\{\Pi_f(\xi), b_f\} \end{aligned} \tag{3.14}$$

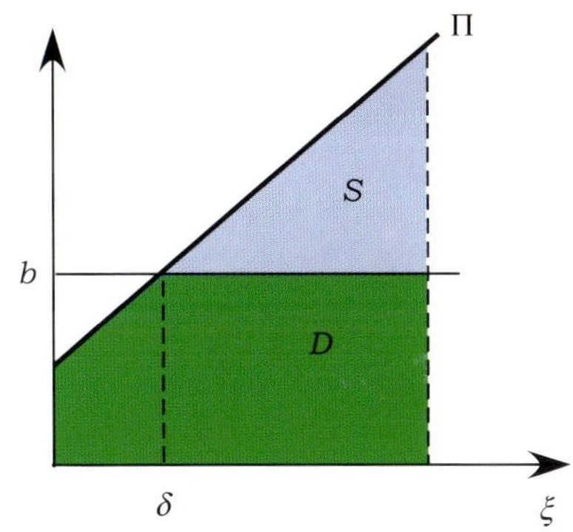

Figure 3.1 Values.

This result is also intuitively appealing because one bond is equivalent to a portfolio of stock with a one dollar payoff for all $\xi \in \Xi \backslash B$ and with a fraction $\Pi_f(\omega)/b_f$ of a dollar payoff for all $\xi \in B$.

By assuming a continuum of states of nature rather than a finite set, the bond and stock market values may be shown in Figure. 3.1.[2] Let δ denote the boundary of the insolvency event, i.e., δ is implicitly defined by the condition $\Pi(\delta) = b$ so that $B = \{\xi | \Pi(\xi) < b\} = [0, \delta)$. The bond or debt value is proportional to the green shaded area in Figure 3.1 and the equity value is proportional to the blue shaded area in the figure.

Call Options

Options are derivative instruments, i.e., instruments that derive their value from other traded instruments. The call option will play a central role in much of the analysis and so is considered here; other options will be considered in subsequent chapters. A call option on an asset gives its holder the right to purchase one share of the asset *then* at an exercise price established *now*. If the call is written on the stock of corporation f then the payoff on the call is

[2]The shaded areas are not quite the values but they are proportional to them. For example, the continuous version of the debt value may be expressed as

$$\begin{aligned} D &= \int_{\Xi} p(\xi) \min\{b, \Pi\}\, d\xi \\ &= p(\beta) \int_{\Xi} \min\{b, \Pi\}\, d\xi \end{aligned}$$

for some β in Ξ; this follows by the intermediate value theorem. A similar comment can be made for the stock value.

$\max\{0, (\Pi_f/N_f) - e_f\}$ where e_f is the exercise price. Let the call option price be c_f. Then

$$c_f = \sum_{\Xi} p(\xi) \max\left\{0, \frac{\Pi_f(\xi)}{N_f} - e_f\right\} \tag{3.15}$$

The value of N_f such options is C_f, where

$$\begin{aligned} C_f &\equiv c_f N_f \\ &= \sum_{\Xi} p(\xi) \max\{0, \Pi_f(\omega) - E_f\} \end{aligned} \tag{3.16}$$

where $E_f = e_f N_f$ is the exercise value. Note that if $b_f = E_f$ then the stock market value of the levered firm is a call option value.

Suggested Problems

1. Define the rate of return for the stock of a levered corporation and show how it changes with leverage.
2. Define the rate of return on the levered zero coupon bond.
3. Define the weighted cost of capital and express it for the levered corporation. How does leverage affect the weighted cost of capital?

Chapter 4

Fisher Separation

Under certainty, Fisher (1930) demonstrated a result that subsequently became known as Fisher separation. In the classic version of the Fisher model, the individual makes a consumption choice and an investment decision to maximize utility subject to a budget constraint. The investment decision requires expenditure *now* and yields a known dollar return *then* based on the size of the investment expenditure. The investment decision alters the temporal income distribution of the individual but that can be compensated for by borrowing or lending in the financial market. It is the ability to compensate for any changes in the temporal distribution of income that generates the Fisher separation result, which says that the investment decision is independent of the individual's preferences for consumption *now* versus *then*. The individual selects that investment decision which maximizes the present value of her income stream and then selects the optimal consumption pair by borrowing or lending in the financial market. Of course, the investment and its return are part of the individual's income stream and so a corollary to the Fisher separation theorem follows immediately and says that the selected investment level is the one that maximizes net present value. Hence, the theorem and corollary have become an important part of corporate finance. The corollary has been used as a theoretical justification for the use of net present value and, in particular, for its use as the corporate objective function.[1]

[1]There is a thread in the literature that deals with the development of a corporate objective function. A few notable examples include. Diamond, P. (1967). "The Role of a Stock Market

Now, consider whether Fisher's results remain intact in this financial market model. In particular, it would be nice to see whether the Fisher separation result holds here and what it implies about an objective function for the publicly held and traded corporation. The corporate objective function has historically been assumed in much of the finance literature; there the assumptions include corporate value, stock value, current shareholder value, etc. One of the advantages of using Fisher's approach to the construction of a financial market model is that the corporate objective function can be derived.

A few cases are considered here in the process of generalizing the Fisher separation theorem and its corollary. The first is in the spirit of the original Fisher model in which a single individual makes the consumption and investment choices. We refer to that individual here as the sole proprietor and show the first separation result. The next case considers what must motivate some of the thinking in corporate finance. In this second case the publicly held and traded corporation is introduced. The corporate decisions are made by a manager who has a salary *now* and *then* and is also paid in corporate stock. In this case, a separation theorem is demonstrated that yields the expected corollary which says that the manager makes all decisions for the corporation to maximize the current shareholder value and another immediate corollary is that maximizing current shareholder value is equivalent to maximizing risk adjusted net present value. Hence, all the expected results are confirmed. Finally, the third case provides a different compensation scheme for the corporate manager. Since stock options were becoming common in the last two decades of the 20th century, the manager is assumed to be given a compensation scheme that provides salary and stock options. A separation result again holds and the corollary in this case yields an objective function which says that the manager makes all decisions on corporate account to maximize the value of the stock option package or equivalently the warrant value. Maximizing warrant value is easily shown to be inconsistent with maximizing net present value.

---

in a General Equilibrium Model with Technological Uncertainty." *American Economic Review* 57: 759–773, Ekern, S. and R. Wilson (1974). "On the Theory of the Firm in an Economy with Incomplete Markets." *Bell Journal of Economics* 5: 171–180, Radner, R. (1974). "A Note on Unanimity of Stockholder's Preferences Among Alternative Production Plans: A Reformulation of the Ekern-Wilson Model." *Bell Journal of Economics* 5: 181–184. This thread of the literature is primarily concerned with the conditions that generate a corporate objective function that yields unanimity among the stakeholders of the corporate. Also see MacMinn, R. (1995). Lecture Notes on Ekern and Wilson's "On the Theory of the Firm in an Economy with Incomplete Markets".

Proprietor

First, consider the classic case of a single proprietorship. Let the proprietor make an investment decision on firm account as well as a portfolio decision on personal account. Let $\Pi_f(I_f, \omega)$ be the earnings of firm f as a function not only of the state of nature but also of the dollar investment I_f. The value of firm f is V_f where

$$V_f = \sum_{\Xi} p(\xi)\Pi_f(I_f, \xi) \tag{4.1}$$

We want to consider whether the proprietor's decision on firm account is separable from her decision on personal account. To allow the proprietor to make the investment decision, let

$$c_{i0} = m_{i0} - \sum_{\Xi} p(\xi)x_i(\xi) - I_f \tag{4.2}$$

and

$$c_{i1}(\xi) = m_{i1}(\xi) + x_i(\xi) + \Pi_f(I_f, \xi) \tag{4.3}$$

The unconstrained form for the proprietor's decision problem is now

$$\text{maximize} \sum_{\Xi} u_i \left(m_{i0} - \sum_{\Xi} p(\xi)x_i(\xi) - I_f,\ m_{i1}(\xi) + x_i(\xi) + \Pi_f(I_f, \xi) \right) \psi_i(\xi) \tag{4.4}$$

Then, in addition to the first order condition for basis stock, or equivalently equation (2.10), we have the condition for an optimal investment level given below

$$-\sum_{\Xi} D_1 u_i \psi_i(\xi) + \sum_{\Xi} D_2 u_i\, D_1 \Pi_f\, \psi_i(\xi) = 0 \tag{4.5}$$

Using equation (2.11), this condition may be rewritten as

$$\sum_{\Xi} p(\xi)\, D_1 \Pi_f = 1 \tag{4.6}$$

Since this condition for an optimal investment level does not depend on either the risk aversion or probability measures of the proprietor, it follows that a Fisher separation result holds here.

Note that the risk adjusted net present value of the investment I_f is $V_f - I_f$. The maximum risk adjusted net present value is implicitly defined by the condition

$$\sum_{\Xi} p(\xi) D_1 \Pi_f - 1 = 0 \tag{4.7}$$

Hence, we see that the proprietor acting in her own interests will select the investment level that maximizes the risk adjusted net present value of the firm. This is the standard corollary to the Fisher separation theorem.

It should be noted that although the investment decision will, other things being equal, change consumption *now*, it can be completely compensated for by altering the position in financial assets. The investment will also change the risk of consumption *then*, but with complete markets that risk can be diversified. This result is particularly important because it generalizes the standard Fisher separation result.

Corporation

Stock compensation scheme

Next, consider the manager of a publicly held and traded corporation. Suppose this manager or CEO makes all decisions on behalf of the corporation as well as personal decisions, i.e., personal portfolio decisions. Call the decisions for the corporation those on corporate account and call the personal decisions those on personal account. Following one of the axioms of economic behavior, we will suppose that the manager makes all decisions in the pursuit of self-interest.

Suppose the manager makes the investment decision for the firm *now* and uses a new stock issue to finance the investment. Let S_f^n denote the value of the new stock issue and let I_f denote the dollar investment. Suppose the firm has issued $N_f + m_f$ shares[2] of stock previously and issues n_f new shares to finance the investment of I_f dollars. Note that the value of the new issue is

$$\begin{aligned} S_f^n &= \sum_{\Xi} p(\xi) \frac{n_f}{N_f + m_f + n_f} \Pi_f(I_f, \xi) \\ &= \frac{n_f}{N_f + m_f + n_f} S_f \end{aligned} \tag{4.8}$$

[2] The m_f shares will be noted later as those shares issued to the corporate manager as part of her compensation scheme.

where S_f is the stock market value, i.e., the value of the new and old issues. The current stockholders have a fractional ownership of

$$1 - \frac{n_f}{N_f + m_f + n_f} = \frac{N_f + m_f}{N_f + m_f + n_f} \tag{4.9}$$

and so the stock market value of the old shareholders' position in the firm is S_f^o, where

$$S_f^o = \frac{N_f + m_f}{N_f + m_f + n_f} S_f \tag{4.10}$$

Now, suppose the manager issues enough new shares to just cover the investment expenditure of I_f dollars, i.e., $S_f^n = I_f$. Finally, note that the old shareholders of the corporation want the manager to act in their interests, i.e., select the investment level to maximize S_f^o.

Suppose the manager is partially paid in corporate stock *now*. Let m_f denote the number of shares held by the manager *now* and *then*.[3] The corporation has $N_f + m_f$ shares outstanding *now* and issues an additional n_f shares to finance the new investment. The manager selects a savings level and portfolio on personal account and an investment level on corporate account to solve the following constrained maximization problem

$$\begin{aligned} &\text{maximize} \int_\Xi u_i(c_{i0}, c_{i1}(\xi))\, d\Psi_i(\xi) \\ &\text{subject to } c_{i0} + \int_\Xi c_{i1}(\xi)\, dP(\xi) = m_{i0} + \int_\Omega m_{i1}(\xi)\, dP(\xi) \\ &\qquad + m_f \int_\Xi \frac{\Pi_f(I_f, \xi)}{N_f + m_f + n_f}\, dP(\xi) \\ &\text{and} \quad \frac{n_f}{N_f + m_f + n_f} \int_\Xi \Pi_f(I_f, \xi)\, dP(\xi) = I_f \end{aligned} \tag{4.11}$$

The last expression in (4.11) is the financing constraint. It determines the number of shares n_f that must be issued *now* to raise the I_f dollars. The penultimate expression in (4.11) is the budget constraint that was represented in previous versions of the problem but with the addition of the last term on the right hand side. That addition to the budget constraint represents part of the compensation in the form of the manager's stake in the equity value of the corporation. The investment decision that the manager makes will have

[3]We could allow the manager to trade shares of corporate stock now without changing the following results as long as the manager has some equity stake in the corporation after trading.

an impact on the random payoff of the corporation and so its value. The problem may also be expressed in reduced form by noting that the financing constraint implicitly defines a function $n_f(I_f)$. Direct calculation yields

$$n_f(I_f) = \frac{I_f}{S_f(I_f) - I_f}(N_f + m_f) \tag{4.12}$$

Substituting this function into the budget constraint and simplifying yields the constrained maximization problem in the following reduced form:

$$\begin{aligned} &\text{maximize} \int_{\Xi} u_i(c_{i0}, c_{i1}(\xi))d\Psi_i(\xi) \\ &\text{subject to } c_{i0} + \int_{\Xi} c_{i1}(\xi)dP(\xi) = m_{i0} + \int_{\Xi} m_{i1}(\xi)dP(\xi) \\ &\qquad + \frac{m_f}{N_f + m_f}(S_f(I_f) - I_f) \end{aligned} \tag{4.13}$$

In this form it is clear that the manager makes decisions on corporate account to maximize $S_f - I_f$. To see this, note that the first order conditions for the decisions on personal account remain the same as those found in equations (2.4) and (2.5); the condition for the investment decision on corporate account is

$$\frac{d}{dI_f}\left(\frac{m_f}{N_f + m_f}(S_f(I_f) - I_f)\right) = \frac{m_f}{N_f + m_f}(S_f'(I_f) - 1) = 0 \tag{4.14}$$

The optimal investment decision is determined by that which makes the marginal stock value equal to the value of the last dollar invested. The decision is separate from the manager's time preferences and risk aversion. Hence, we have a Fisher separation result for the publicly held and traded corporation. It may also be observed that the manager selects the investment level to maximize the risk adjusted net present value, or equivalently, the current shareholder value since $S_f - I_f = S_f - S_f^n = S_f^o$.

Stock option compensation scheme

The compensation of the manager may take a variety of forms. Each should yield a separation result with the corresponding corollary that specifies the objective function. To see this, suppose the manager is partially paid in stock options *now*. Each option gives the manager the right to purchase one share of corporate stock *then* at an exercise price of e_f dollars. Suppose the manager is paid with m_f options *now*. The corporation has N_f shares outstanding *now* and issues an additional m_f shares *then* if the manager exercises the options. Without loss of generality, suppose the firm issues bonds *now* to cover its investment expenditure. The manager selects a consumption plan equivalently portfolio on personal account and an investment level on corporate account to solve the following constrained maximization problem

$$\begin{aligned} &\text{maximize} \int_\Xi u_i(c_{i0}, c_{i1}(\xi))\, d\Psi_i(\xi) \\ &\text{subject to } c_{i0} + \int_\Xi c_{i1}(\xi)\, dP(\xi) = m_{i0} + \int_\Xi m_{i1}(\xi)\, dP(\xi) \\ &\qquad + \int_\Xi \max\left\{0, \frac{m_f}{N_f + m_f}(\Pi_f(I_f, \xi) \right. \\ &\qquad \left. + e_f m_f - b_f) - e_f m_f \right\} dP(\xi) \\ &\text{and} \quad \int_\Xi \min\{\Pi_f(I_f, \xi), b_f\}\, dP(\xi) = I_f \end{aligned} \tag{4.15}$$

The last expression in the problem is the financing constraint. It determines the promised payment b_f on the debt issued *now* necessary to raise the I_f dollars for the investment. The problem may also be expressed in reduced form by noting that the financing constraint implicitly defines a function $b_f(I_f)$. Substituting this function into the budget constraint and simplifying yields the constrained maximization problem in the following reduced form:

$$\begin{aligned} &\text{maximize} \int_\Xi u_i(c_{i0}, c_{i1}(\xi))\, d\Psi_i(\xi) \\ &\text{subject to } c_{i0} + \int_\Xi c_{i1}(\xi)\, dP(\xi) = m_{i0} + \int_\Xi m_{i1}(\xi)\, dP(\xi) + W_f(I_f) \end{aligned} \tag{4.16}$$

where W_f represents the value of the stock option package, or equivalently, the warrant value. The warrant value may be equivalently expressed as

$$W_f(I_f) = \int_\Xi \max\left\{0, \frac{m_f}{N_f + m_f}(\Pi_f(I_f, \xi) - b_f(I_f)) - \left(1 - \frac{m_f}{N_f + m_f}\right) E_f\right\} dP \tag{4.17}$$

where $E_f = e_f m_f$ is the gross exercise value. It becomes clear in (4.16) that the manager will make decisions on corporate account to maximize the warrant value. Hence, we have another Fisher separation result for the publicly held and traded corporation. It should also now be clear that the manager paid in stock options does not have the incentive to make decisions that maximize current shareholder value.

To note the difference in incentives, consider the investment choices made by managers paid in stock versus stock options where the latter are not too deeply in the money, i.e., there is some positive probability that the options will not be in the money when they vest *then*. The incentives for the corporate manager paid in stock options become clear when we compare the investment decision of managers with different compensation schemes. Suppose, for example, that one corporate manager is paid in stock and another is paid in stock options. Suppose they have identical investment frontiers and both can finance their choices with safe debt.[4] The manager paid in stock options selects the investment level to maximize $W(I)$ and so the first order condition is

$$W'(I^w) = \frac{m_f}{N_f + m_f} \int_{\gamma}^{\omega} (D_1\Pi(I^w, \xi) - b')\, dP(\xi) = 0 \tag{4.18}$$

where γ is the boundary of the exercise event and I^w denotes the investment level implicitly defined by (4.18). The stock market value of the corporation that finances with safe debt is

$$S(I) = \int_0^{\omega} (\Pi(I, \xi) - b(I))\, dP(\xi) \tag{4.19}$$

and the manager paid in stock selects the investment level to maximize $S(I)$; the first order condition is

$$S'(I^s) = \int_0^{\omega} (D_1\Pi(I^s, \xi) - b')\, dP(\xi) = 0 \tag{4.20}$$

Now to make a comparison of I^w and I^s, suppose the investment frontier satisfies the derivative properties $D_2\Pi > 0$ and $D_{21}\Pi$ so that the Principle of Increasing Uncertainty (PIU) holds. Roughly put, this means that the risk of the investment increases in the size of the investment.[5] Evaluating the first order condition (4.20) at I^w yields the following

$$\begin{aligned} S'(I^w) &= \int_0^{\gamma} (D_1\Pi(I^w, \xi) - b')\, dP(\xi) + \int_{\gamma}^{\omega} (D_1\Pi(I^w, \xi) - b')\, dP(\xi) \\ &= \int_0^{\gamma} (D_1\Pi(I^w, \xi) - b')\, dP(\xi) \\ &< 0 \end{aligned} \tag{4.21}$$

[4]This assumption of safe debt is only made for convenience and simplicity. It does make the function $b(I)$ implicitly defined by $D(b) = I$ linear, i.e., b' is a constant equal to one plus the safe rate of return.

[5]See Leland, H. (1972). "Theory of the Firm Facing Uncertain Demand." *American Economic Review* **62**: 278–291, MacMinn, R. D. and A. Holtmann (1983). "Technological Uncertainty and the Theory of the Firm." *Southern Economic Journal* **50**: 120–136. Leland defines the principle of increasing uncertainty using the derivative properties noted here and MacMinn shows that after correcting for the change in the mean of the payoff distribution, the increase in risk can be interpreted as a Rothschild–Stiglitz increase in risk or equivalently a mean preserving spread of the payoff distribution, i.e., see Rothschild, M. and J. E. Stiglitz (1970). "Increasing Risk: I. A Definition." *Journal of Economic Theory* **2**: 225–243.

The second equality in (4.21) follows by (4.18) and the inequality follows by the PIU. Equivalently, the inequality follows because $D_1\Pi$ is monotone increasing and $D_1\Pi - b'$ negative for some state $\xi > \gamma$ makes the integral on the right hand side of the second equality negative. Hence, the manager paid in stock options selects a greater investment level, i.e., $I^w > I^s$. The manager paid in stock options takes on more risk than the manager paid in stock.

Remarks

Each result here shows that the basic intuition of the certainty version of the Fisher model continues to hold in this setting. The proprietor example is the simplest extension of the Fisher result but the corporate manager examples are more relevant. As long as the manager can diversify her portfolio on personal account, the motivation for decisions on corporate account will be driven by the most basic axiom in economics, i.e., more is preferred to less. It should be noted that if the manager is paid with stock, then there is an alignment of interests with current shareholders and, what is more, the maximization of current shareholder value is equivalent to the net present value rule for investment choices. If the manager is paid with stock options, then there is no general alignment of interests with shareholders. During the last two decades of the 20th century, the seemingly unassailable argument for stock options was that the options would only be in the money if the share price increased and so the connection between options and incentives was supposed to be obvious. That flawed logic, of course, ignored the risk taking incentives and the consequent impact on value. The more important observation here, however, is the general observation that the corollary to each Fisher separation result yields a corporate objective function. Hence, the objective function is endogenous.

Suggested Problems

1. Suppose the manager's compensation is a known salary *now* and *then* plus a bonus. Consider a few ways to construct a bonus scheme and derive the manager's objective function for each.
2. Suppose the firm is producing a good or service and the manager must make a production decision q. Let $\Pi(q,\xi)$ be the corporate payoff given the production decision q. Suppose the manager is paid in stock. If the firm is levered from a previous debt issue and b is the promised payment on

that debt, then derive the condition for an optimal production decision. Compare the optimal production decision for the case in which the risk of insolvency is zero versus that in which it is positive.

3. Claim: The manager paid with stock options has an incentive to takeover a target firm even if the net present value is non-positive. Prove it or provide a counter example.

Chapter 5

More Values

In this chapter we want to value debt and equity using options and consider how to value bond-warrant packages and convertible bond packages. The subscript f for the corporation will be understood but not included here for simplicity. The corporate value is the value of the firm's debt plus equity and will be denoted by V hereafter.

Call Options

A call option on an asset gives its holder the right to purchase one share of the asset at the end of the period at an established exercise price. If the call is written on the stock of corporation f then the payoff on the call is $\max\{0, (\Pi/N) - e\}$. We have shown that the price of the call option is c where

$$c = \int_{\Xi} \max\left\{0, \frac{\Pi(\xi)}{N} - e\right\} dP \tag{5.1}$$

If the corporation issues N call options then $C = cN$ is the market value of its options. Therefore we have

$$C = \int_{\Xi} \max\{0, \Pi(\xi) - E\}\, dP \tag{5.2}$$

where $E = eN$. Next, recall that we have shown that the stock market value of a levered corporation is $S(b)$ where

$$S(b) = \int_{\Xi} \max\{0, \Pi(\xi) - b\}\, dP = C \tag{5.3}$$

Therefore the stock market value of the levered corporation may be interpreted as the market value of a call option on the firm where b is the exercise value. Also recall that the value of the corporation's debt issue is

$$D(b) = \int_{\Xi} \min\{\Pi(\xi), b\}\, dP \tag{5.4}$$

Since $\min\{\Pi, b\} = \Pi - \max\{0, \Pi - b\}$, it follows that the corporate debt value may also be expressed as the value of the corporation minus the value of a call option on the corporation, i.e.,

$$\begin{aligned} D(b) &= \int_{\Xi} [\Pi - \max\{0, \Pi - b\}]\, dP \\ &= \int_{\Xi} \Pi\, dP - \int_{\Xi} \max\{0, \Pi - b\}\, dP \\ &= V - C \end{aligned} \tag{5.5}$$

Hence, it is possible to express the value of the levered corporation in terms of a call option. The bondholders purchase the asset, i.e., firm, and sell a call option on the asset to stockholders.

Put Options

It is also possible to express the corporate debt and equity issues in terms of puts. A put option on an asset gives its holder the right to sell the asset at the end of the period at an established exercise price. If the put is written on the stock of the corporation, then the payoff on the put is $\max\{0, e - (\Pi/N)\}$. Then the market value of the put option is p where

$$p = \int_{\Xi} \max\left\{0, e - \frac{\Pi(\xi)}{N}\right\} dP \tag{5.6}$$

Note that if N puts are issued then the value of the put issue is

$$P \equiv pN = \int_{\Xi} \max\{0, E - \Pi\}\, dP \tag{5.7}$$

where now E is the price at which the stock issue of the firm is sold, i.e., its exercise value.

If we interpret the debt payment b as the exercise value, then we may observe that the stock market value of the levered corporation is the risk adjusted value of the firm's earnings net of bond payments plus the value of a put option on the firm. To see this, note that $\max\{0, \Pi - b\} = \Pi - b + \max\{0, b - \Pi\}$. It follows that

$$\begin{aligned} S(b) &= \int_{\Xi} (\Pi(\xi) - b)\, dP + \int_{\Xi} \max\{0, b - \Pi(\xi)\}\, dP \\ &= V - B(b) + P \end{aligned} \tag{5.8}$$

where $B(b)$ is the value of a safe debt issue. The stock market value of the levered firm is the value of the firm minus the risk adjusted present value of the exercise price plus the value of the put. Equivalently, the stock market value of the levered firm is its corporate value minus the value of a safe debt issue plus the value of the put. It is apparent that the put value may be interpreted as the value of the shareholders' limited liability. Similarly, since $\min\{\Pi, b\} = b - \max\{0, b - \Pi\}$, the corporate debt value is

$$\begin{aligned} D(b) &= \int_{\Xi} b\, dP - \int_{\Xi} \max\{0, b - \Pi(\xi)\}\, dP \\ &= B(b) - P \end{aligned} \tag{5.9}$$

Hence the debt value is the risk adjusted present value of the exercise price minus the value of the put. Equivalently, it is the value of safe debt minus the value of the put.

Bonds with Attached Warrants

Next, consider the value of a bond-warrant package. Suppose each bond is issued with a warrant which gives its owner the right to purchase $\gamma(N+n)/b$ shares of stock at an exercise price of e per share of common stock. N is the number of shares *now*, while n is the number of new shares which must be issued *then* if the warrants are exercised. The fraction γ is simply $n/(N+n)$. Note that a warrant is simply a call option. The payoff on a warrant is

$$\max\left\{0, \gamma \frac{N+n}{b}\left(\frac{\Pi - b + E}{N+n} - e\right)\right\} \tag{5.10}$$

and so the payoff on the entire warrant issue is

$$b \max\left\{0, \gamma \frac{N+n}{b}\left(\frac{\Pi - b + E}{N+n} - e\right)\right\} = \max\{0, \gamma\left(\Pi - b + E\right) - E\} \tag{5.11}$$

where we define E as the exercise value of the warrant issue, i.e., $E = e\gamma(N+n) = en$. Then it follows easily that the market value of the warrant

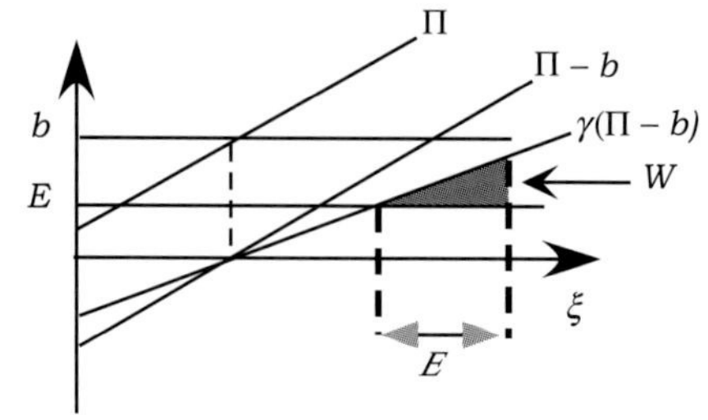

Figure 5.1 Warrant value.

issue is

$$W(b, e, \gamma) = \int_{\Xi} \max\{0, \gamma(\Pi - b) - E\}\, dP \tag{5.12}$$

Note that the warrant is only exercised in the event that the firm is solvent. It follows that the bond-warrant holders have a payoff of $\min\{\Pi, b\} + \max\{0, \gamma(\Pi - b) - E\}$. Letting $D(b, e, \gamma)$ denote the market value of the bond-warrant package, note that

$$\begin{aligned} D(b, e, \gamma) &= \int_{\Xi} \min\{\Pi(\xi), b\}\, dP + \int_{\Xi} \max\{0, \gamma(\Pi(\xi) - b) - E\}\, dP \\ &= D(b) + W(b, e, \gamma) \end{aligned} \tag{5.13}$$

as shown in Figure 5.2. Observe that (5.13) yields the result that the market value of the package is equivalent to the value of a simple debt contract plus the value of the warrant. The stockholders in this corporation have a payoff $\max\{0, \Pi - b\} - \max\{0, \gamma\Pi - b) - E\}$. Hence, letting $S(b, e, \gamma)$ denote the stock market value of the firm with the bond-warrant package, we obtain

$$\begin{aligned} S(b, e, \gamma) &= \int_{\Xi} \max\{0, \Pi - b\}\, dP - \int_{\Xi} \max\{0, \gamma(\Pi - b) - E\}\, dP \\ &= S(b) - W(b, e, \gamma) \end{aligned} \tag{5.14}$$

Hence, the stock market value of the firm with a bond-warrant package is equivalent to the stock market value of the firm with the simple debt contract minus the value of the warrant as shown in Figure 5.2. The 1958 Modigliani–Miller Theorem provided irrelevance result for corporate capital structure that says that the value of the levered firm equals that of the unlevered. Letting b and n denote the size of the debt and equity issues, respectively, the theorem says that $V(b, 0) = V(0, n)$ as will be demonstrated in the next chapter. It may be noted that a generalization of the 1958 Modigliani–Miller Theorem follows here, since $V(b, e, \gamma, 0) = V(b, 0) = V(0, n)$.

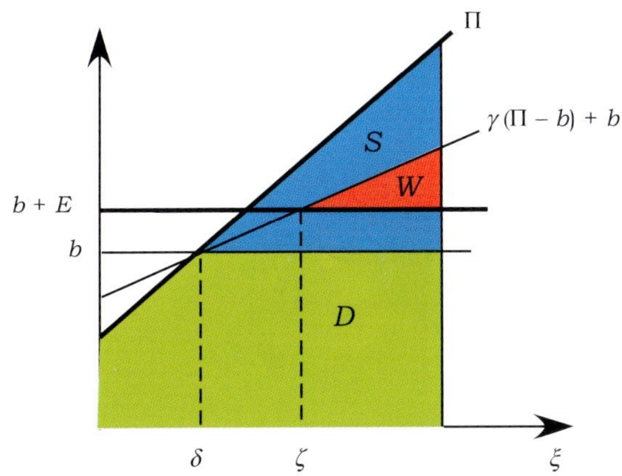

Figure 5.2 Stock value with a warrant issue.

Convertible Bonds

Next, consider convertible bonds. The convertible bond is a bond that includes a call option. It is similar to a bond with an attached warrant. The most obvious difference between the two is that the convertible bond owner surrenders the bond in order to exercise the option, while the bond-warrant owner surrenders cash in order to exercise the option. There are other differences including the fact that most warrants are detachable, while the option in the bond-call option package cannot be detached, and the fact that warrants, unlike many convertibles, cannot be called.

The feature of convertible bonds that makes them operational is the conversion ratio. Suppose that the bondholders acquire a fraction of the firm's equity upon conversion and let the conversion ratio be $\theta = \gamma(N+n)/b$, where $\gamma \in (0,1)$ and as before n is the number of shares that must be issued *then* if bondholders convert to stock. The payoff on a convertible bond is

$$\max\left\{\theta\frac{\Pi}{N+n}, \min\left\{1, \frac{\Pi}{b}\right\}\right\} = \max\left\{\gamma\frac{\Pi}{b}, \min\left\{1, \frac{\Pi}{b}\right\}\right\} \tag{5.15}$$

and the payoff on the convertible bond issue is

$$b\max\left\{\gamma\frac{\Pi}{b}, \min\left\{1, \frac{\Pi}{b}\right\}\right\} = \max\{\gamma\Pi, \min\{\Pi, b\}\} \tag{5.16}$$

Now, observe that the payoff may be equivalently expressed as

$$\begin{aligned}\max\{\gamma\Pi, \min\{\Pi, b\}\} &= \min\{\Pi, b\} + \max\{0, \gamma\Pi - \min\{\Pi, b\}\} \\ &= \min\{\Pi, b\} + \max\{0, \gamma\Pi - b\}\end{aligned} \tag{5.17}$$

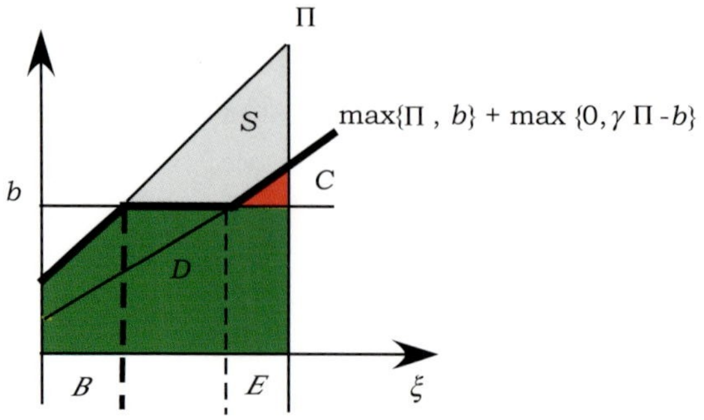

Figure 5.3 Call option value.

Therefore, letting $D(b, \gamma)$ denote the value of the convertible debt issue, it follows that

$$\begin{aligned} D(b,\gamma) &= \int_{\Xi} \min\{\Pi(\xi), b\}\, dP + \int_{\Xi} \max\{0, \gamma\Pi(\xi) - b\}\, dP \\ &= D(b) + C(b,\gamma) \end{aligned} \tag{5.18}$$

Hence, the value of convertible debt is simply the value of straight debt plus the value of a call option. Since the bonds are converted if and only if the firm is solvent, we may note that the payoff to stockholders is

$$\begin{aligned} \min\{\max\{0, \Pi - b\}, (1-\gamma)\Pi\} &= \max\{0, \Pi - b\} \\ &\quad - \max\{0, \Pi - b - (1-\gamma)\Pi\} \\ &= \max\{0, \Pi - b\} - \max\{0, \gamma\Pi - b\} \end{aligned} \tag{5.19}$$

Therefore, letting $S(b, \gamma)$ denote the stock market value of the firm with convertible debt, we obtain

$$S(b, \gamma) = S(b) - C(b, \gamma) \tag{5.20}$$

Again, it may be noted that the 1958 Modigliani–Miller irrelevance result holds, i.e., $V(b, \gamma, 0) = V(b, 0) = V(0, n)$. In fact the irrelevance result follows by noting that the market values of the financial instruments are simply the risk adjusted present values of the areas shown in Figure 5.3.

Suggested Problems

1. Consider a bond-warrant package. Specify the payoff on the bond-warrant and derive the value.

2. Suppose the corporation faces a random property loss of L dollars where $L : \Xi \to R$ and that the corporation may purchase insurance *now* for a premium of $p_i(d)$ given a deductible of d dollars, i.e., the insurance contract pays zero up to the deductible and *then* the loss minus the deductible for all larger losses. Provide an expression for the value of the insurance premium.

Chapter 6

Corporate Finance Theorems

Once the publicly held and traded corporation determines operating and investment strategies, the firm may make a number of financial decisions that have an impact on the value of its financial claims.[1] If the corporation raises funds for its investments externally, then it makes a capital structure decision that affects the value of its debt and equity. If the firm raises funds for its investments internally, then it makes a dividend policy decision. The dividend decision is not independent of the capital structure decision; a particular dividend decision may require a capital structure decision if not all the funds for investment can be raised internally. Here, we consider some of the classic theorems in corporate finance that answer the question of how these decisions affect the value of the corporation. In the absence of conflict of interest problems, the theorems show that in a competitive financial market system, the net present value of the alternative financing schemes is zero and so the composition of the corporation's contract set is irrelevant.

Classic Theorems

1958 Modigliani–Miller Theorem: If the financial markets are competitive, *ceteris paribus*, the value of the levered firm equals that of the unlevered firm.

[1]The operating, investment and financing decisions are not typically independent. The dependence of these decisions is a topic considered in the next chapter. The classic theorems take operating and investment decisions as given.

The *ceteris paribus* is added here because it is implicit in the original work; no operating or investment decisions are made in conjunction with the capital structure decision. Once the corporation has decided to raise funds externally, it may alter the amount it raises in the bond market versus the stock market. The 1958 Modigliani–Miller Theorem shows that, although an alteration in the size of the debt issue changes the value of the debt versus the equity, it does not change the total market value of the corporation. Modigliani and Miller considered the case in which the debt issue is safe, i.e., $\Pi(I,\xi) \geq b$ for all $\xi \in \Xi$, or equivalently $P\{\Pi = b\} = 1$.[2] Let (b,n) denote the financing pair where b is the promised payment *then* on a zero coupon bond issue and n is the number of new shares issued *now*. Let $V(b,n)$ represent the value of the corporation given its financing decision (b,n). The firm is incorporated and so has shares outstanding but will be assumed to be unlevered prior to this financing decision. Consider two cases. Let the first be that in which the firm raises the requisite funds for investment with just a debt issue. In this case, the value of the levered firm is $V(b,0) = D(b) + S(b,0)$. Let the second case be that in which the firm raises the necessary funds for investment with just a new stock issue; in this case, the unlevered firm is $V(0,n) = S(0,n)$. Observe that the unlevered corporate or equivalently stock value is

$$\begin{aligned} V(0,n) &= S^n(0,n) + S^o(0,n) \\ &= \frac{n}{n+N} S(0,n) + \frac{N}{n+N} S(0,n) \\ &= S(0,n) \\ &= \int_\Xi \Pi(I,\xi)\, dP \end{aligned} \tag{6.1}$$

where as previously S^n and S^o represent new and old shareholder value, respectively. Now observe that the levered value is

$$\begin{aligned} V(b,0) &\equiv D(b) + S(b,0) \\ &= \int_\Xi b\, dP + \int_\Xi (\Pi(I,\xi) - b)\, dP \\ &= \int_\Xi \Pi(I,\xi)\, dP \\ &= V(0,n) \end{aligned} \tag{6.2}$$

[2]The subscript f for the corporation is to be understood here but is not included for simplicity.

Hence, the 1958 Theorem follows rather easily and, of course, says that the value of the corporation is independent of its capital structure.

A result on the weighted cost of capital is often stated as a corollary. The weighted cost of capital is defined as follows:

$$R_w = \frac{S}{V}R_s + \frac{D}{V}R_d \tag{6.3}$$

where R_s is the random rate of return on equity and R_d is the random rate of return on debt. Recall that the rates of return are

$$R_s = \frac{\max\{0, \Pi - b\}}{S} - 1, \quad R_d = \frac{\min\{\Pi, b\}}{D} - 1 \tag{6.4}$$

Given safe debt,[3] it follows that the weighted cost of capital is

$$\begin{aligned} R_w &= \frac{S}{V}\left(\frac{\Pi - b}{S} - 1\right) + \frac{D}{V}\left(\frac{b}{D} - 1\right) \\ &= \frac{S}{V}\left(\frac{\Pi - b}{S}\right) + \frac{D}{V}\left(\frac{b}{D}\right) - 1 \\ &= \frac{\Pi}{V} - 1 \end{aligned} \tag{6.5}$$

Observe that this weighted cost is independent of the corporation's capital structure.

Of course, it has also been observed by some authors that the result need not be restricted to the case in which debt is safe, e.g., Stiglitz (1969) and Baron (1976). When the corporate debt issue is risky the bond payoff is $\min\{\Pi, b\}$ while the equity payoff is $\max\{0, \Pi - b\}$. Then

$$\begin{aligned} V(b, 0) &= \int_{\Xi} \min\{\Pi(I, \xi), b\}\, dP + \int_{\Xi} \max\{0, \Pi(I, \xi) - b\}\, dP \\ &= \int_{\Xi} \Pi(I, \xi)\, dP \\ &= V(0, n) \end{aligned} \tag{6.6}$$

This is a slight generalization of the 1958 Modigliani–Miller Theorem; it simply allows for the possibility that the firm becomes insolvent *then*.

Although the 1958 Modigliani–Miller Theorem was designed to show that the corporation's capital structure decisions are not value increasing or decreasing, it has become apparent that the theorem is far more general. If, following Alchian and Demsetz (1972), we view the firm as a nexus of

[3]This cost of capital result obviously holds for risky debt too.

contracts then the question of an optimal composition of contracts naturally arises. The 1958 Theorem limits the contract set to debt and equity and says that the composition of the contract set is irrelevant. The theorem, however, generalizes quite easily to more complex contract sets and still provides an irrelevance result that says that the composition of the contract set is irrelevant. For example, consider a futures contract. Let Φ denote unit payoff on the stock index and let f denote the futures price. The payoff on the futures position is $\phi(f - \Phi)$, where ϕ is the number of futures purchased. The corporate payoff is $\Pi + \phi(f - \Phi)$ and the value of the hedged firm is equal to the value of the unhedged firm, i.e.,

$$\begin{aligned} S(0, n, \phi) &= \int_{\Xi} (\Pi(I, \xi) + \phi(f - \Phi))\, dP \\ &= S(0, n, 0) + \phi \int_{\Xi} (f - \Phi)\, dP \\ &= S(0, n, 0) \end{aligned} \tag{6.7}$$

This follows because the risk adjusted present value of the futures price equals the risk adjusted present value of the unit payoff. This line of analysis will be pursued in the risk management chapter.

1961 Miller–Modigliani Theorem: If the financial markets are competitive, *ceteris paribus*, the value of the corporation paying dividends equals that of the corporation paying no dividends.

Holding the corporate investment decision fixed, the dividend policy question may be understood as the question of whether the corporation should raise funds internally or externally. Equivalently, dividend policy may be understood as the question of whether investors would prefer the corporation to keep its earnings and invest them or pay them out *now* as dividends. In a competitive market system with no taxes, we show that the 1958 Modigliani–Miller result on the irrelevance of the firm's capital structure may be combined with the 1961 Miller–Modigliani result on the irrelevance of dividend policy, to show that the source and type of funds used to finance an investment project have no effect on the value of the corporation.[4]

Consider introducing a dividend *now*. Let d denote the total number of dollars in dividends paid by the firm *now* to holders of record in proportion to their ownership of the firm. Since we want to consider pre-dividend values, suppose that the sequence of events is as follows: Firms announce their dividend policies and trading occurs in the bond and stock markets; then

[4]Source refers to external versus internal funds while type refers to the characteristics of the issue, e.g., debt or equity.

dividends are paid and consumption *now* takes place. The financing and dividend decisions may be represented by the triple (b, n, d), where b represents the face value of a debt issue, n represents the number of new shares issued, and d represents the dividend paid *now*. Let $S(b, 0, d)$ denote the stock market value of the firm *now*, given that the firm pays a dividend and issues debt to finance its investment. Similarly, let $S(0, 0, 0)$ denote the stock market value of the firm which pays no dividend and finances its investment with retained earnings.[5] Finally, let $S(0, n, d)$ denote the stock market value of the firm that pays a dividend and finances its investment by issuing new equity. Then it follows trivially that $S(b, 0, d) = S(0, 0, 0) = S(0, n, d) - d$, as the following analysis shows.

Now, consider the dividend decision. Let the pair $(\pi, \Pi(I, \xi))$ denote the firm's earnings *now* and *then*, respectively. Suppose the firm's investment decision is fixed so that its earnings *then* are not affected by dividend policy. Further, suppose that π is sufficient to cover the firm's investment expenditure *now* if it is retained, i.e., letting I denote the fixed investment expenditure *now*, we suppose $\pi - I = 0$. If earnings *now* are not retained then the firm must issue equity or debt to cover its fixed investment expenditure. If the firm selects a dividend *now* of $d > 0$ and issues debt to finance its investment then the stock value is

$$\begin{aligned} S^o(b, 0, d) &= d + \int_{\Xi} [\Pi(I, \xi) - b]\, dP \\ &= \int_{\Xi} \Pi(I, \xi)\, dP \\ &= S^o(0, 0, 0) \end{aligned} \tag{6.8}$$

This result follows since the value of the debt issue equals the value of the dividend payment, i.e.,

$$D(b) = \int_{\Xi} b\, dP = I = \pi = d \tag{6.9}$$

This result says that the stock value of the firm paying a dividend and raising the dollars needed for investment with a debt issue is the same as the stock value of the firm paying no dividend and raising all the dollars internally. Note that the stock market values here refer to both the total stock value

[5] In this section of the paper, we will assume that the firm has earnings *now* denoted by π_{f0}. Of course, there is no uncertainty about the firm's current earnings. Since the firm pays dividends out of current earnings, this will allow us to specify a dividend now for the investors, in two of the three financing methods considered here.

and current shareholder value because there are no new equity holders; in the next case the distinction becomes important. Suppose the firm pays a dividend and issues new equity to finance the investment. Then the current shareholder value is

$$\begin{aligned} S^o(0,n,d) &= S(0,n,d) - S^n(0,n,d) \\ &= d + \int_{\Xi} \Pi(I,\xi)\,dP - I \\ &= S^o(0,0,0) \end{aligned} \tag{6.10}$$

This result follows since the value of the new equity issue equals the value of the dividend payment, i.e.,

$$S^n(0,n,d) = I = \pi = d \tag{6.11}$$

This result says that the current shareholder value of the firm paying a dividend and raising the dollars needed for investment with a new equity issue is the same as the stock value of the firm paying no dividend and raising all the dollars internally. Equations (6.8) and (6.10) suffice to demonstrate the 1961 Miller–Modigliani Theorem on the irrelevance of dividend policy. It may also be noted that the 1958 Modigliani–Miller Theorem follows as a corollary. Observe that the corporate value given the financing triple is $V(b,n,d)$; then

$$\begin{aligned} V(b,0,d) &\equiv D(b) + S(b,0,d) \\ &= d + \int_{\Xi} \Pi(I,\xi)\,dP \\ &= S(0,n,d) \\ &= V(0,n,d) \end{aligned} \tag{6.12}$$

Note that (6.12) holds dividend policy fixed and shows that the value of the levered firm equals that of the unlevered firm.

1963 Modigliani–Miller Theorem: If the financial markets are competitive and corporations are taxed, *ceteris paribus*, the value of the levered firm equals that of the unlevered firm plus the value of the debt tax shield.

In this extension of the 1958 capital structure result, Modigliani and Miller consider an economy in which individual investors are not taxed but corporations are taxed at a rate t. Since interest payments on the firm's debt issue are deductible, the corporation can limit its tax payment to the Government by increasing the size of its debt issue and so reducing the corporation's taxable income. This motivates the 1963 Modigliani–Miller result which says that the value of the levered corporation equals the value of the unlevered corporation plus the value of the corporate debt tax shelter. Of course, in its strictest form this result implicitly assumes that any redundant deductions can be preserved without cost through merger, leasing, or other financial transactions. Since the interest payments on debt are tax deductible we introduce coupon bearing bonds here and let r denote the coupon rate. Then the corporation's taxable income is $\Pi - rb$ where b is now the face value of the debt instrument. Letting T denote the corporation's tax liability, we have

$$T = t\max\{0, \Pi - rb\} \tag{6.13}$$

The value of the tax liability in the absence of insolvency risk is

$$\begin{aligned}\int_{\Xi} t\max\{0, \Pi - rb\}\, dP &= t\int_{\Xi} (\Pi - rb)\, dP \\ &= tV - t\frac{rb}{1+r}\end{aligned} \tag{6.14}$$

For the unlevered firm, the right hand side of (6.14) reduces to tV. The return to bondholders is

$$\min\{(1+r)b, \Pi - T\} \tag{6.15}$$

while the return to shareholders is

$$\max\{0, \Pi - \min\{(1+r)b, \Pi - T\} - T\} \tag{6.16}$$

Given no insolvency risk the returns to bondholders and shareholders are $(1+r)b$ and

$$\Pi - (1+r)b - t(\Pi - rb) = (1-t)\Pi - (1 + r(1-t))b \tag{6.17}$$

respectively. Suppose the bond was issued at par so that $\int_{\Xi} dP = \frac{1}{1+r}$[6]; then given no insolvency risk the value of the debt issue is

$$\begin{aligned}D &= \int_{\Xi} (1+r)\, b\, dP \\ &= b\end{aligned} \tag{6.18}$$

and the levered value of the equity is S^{ℓ} where

$$S^{\ell} = \int_{\Xi} ((1-t)\Pi - (1 + r(1-t))b)\, dP \tag{6.19}$$

[6]The left hand side is the sum of the basis stock prices and is always equal the discount factor for a safe asset that is shown on the right hand side; the only difference here is that the interest rate on the right hand side is also the coupon rate.

Hence, letting V^ℓ and V^u denote the levered and unlevered corporate values, respectively, the levered corporate value is

$$\begin{aligned} V^\ell &= D + S^\ell \\ &= \int_\Xi (1+r)b\,dP + \int_\Xi ((1-t)\Pi - (1 + r(1-t))b)\,dP \\ &= \int_\Xi ((1-t)\Pi + trb)\,dP \\ &= V^u + trb\int_\Xi dP \\ &= V^u + t\frac{rb}{1+r} \\ &= V^u + C \end{aligned} \tag{6.20}$$

Figure 6.1 is a simple demonstration of the 1963 Theorem. It says that the value of the levered corporation is the risk adjusted present value of the after tax cash flow or equivalently the value of the unlevered corporation plus the present value of the debt tax shelter. The corporation can increase value by levering up but as Figure 6.1 demonstrates, the corporation risks loosing tax credits if the leverage increases to a point at which the debt introduces insolvency risk. The areas labeled T and C in Figure 6.1 represent the value of the corporate tax liability and debt tax shelter, respectively. The figure also makes it quite clear that the increase in corporate value is achieved by reducing the value of the tax liability. Hence, there is no change in value. There is only a redistribution of value.

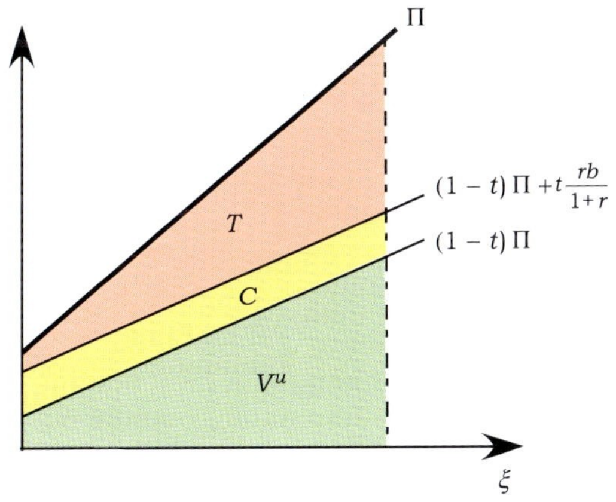

Figure 6.1 The 1963 Miller–Modigliani Theorem.

1977 Miller Theorem: If the financial markets are competitive and both corporations and investors are taxed, the equilibrium value of the levered firm equals that of the unlevered firm.

Miller argued that, in an economy with investors in different personal tax brackets and with limitations on short selling, corporations will attempt to increase value by issuing bonds but the bond rate of interest will be driven up to the point at which the net present value of the tax shelter is zero. Equivalently, he argued that, in such an economy, the value of the levered firm will equal the value of the unlevered firm. Miller demonstrated the result under certainty. Also see DeAngelo and Masulis (1980) and MacMinn and Martin (1988) for discussion.

1980 DeAngelo–Masulis Theorem: If the financial markets are competitive but corporations cannot protect tax credits and shields without cost, the equilibrium value of the levered firm equals that of the unlevered firm plus the values of the tax shields and credits; in some market equilibria the levered value plus the shields and credits exceeds the unlevered value.

DeAngelo and Masulis demonstrated Miller's result under uncertainty in a complete market model and then went on to show that, by modifying the tax treatment of corporations, an optimal capital structure can be determined for the firm. DeAngelo and Masulis, however, assumed that the total debt payment could be deducted from corporate earnings in determining taxable income.

Remarks

There are a few more classic theorems in corporate finance that are considered in subsequent chapters. The risk-shifting or equivalently asset substitution problem will be considered in Chapter 7 while the pecking order theorem will be considered in Chapter 8.

Suggested Problems

1. Suppose the levered firm does have some insolvency risk so that the returns to bondholders and stockholders are as given in (6.15) and (6.16), respectively. Does a generalized version of the 1963 Theorem hold? Specify the levered corporate value and discuss it.
2. Suppose investors have tax rates t_i on the interest from corporate bonds they may hold and that some investors have tax rates higher and lower than the corporate tax rate. Derive the supply and demand for bond funds. Use these functions to demonstrate the Miller 1977 Theorem.

Chapter 7

Agency Problems

In this chapter, two of the classic agency problems are considered. The first is the risk-shifting or equivalently the asset substitution problem. It incorporates the simplest type of asymmetric information problem in the form of a hidden action taken by corporate management. The firm issues bonds to finance its investment in either one of two mutually exclusive projects. One of the projects is riskier than the other and the investors do not know which project the firm will select. Hence, there is a hidden action. The riskier project yields a smaller bondholder return. The investors must be able to predict which project the firm will select in order to value the bonds and they are aware of the firm's ability to shift risk to bondholders if the bonds are not appropriately valued. Given these circumstances there can be a conflict between stockholders and bondholders with respect to project selection. Green (1984) considered a version of this problem and showed how convertible bonds could be used to solve the problem as will be done here.

The second agency problem is the under-investment problem. The classic statement of the problem is that the firm is currently levered and is considering financing for another project. Although the new financing is appropriately valued in financial markets, the benefits of the new project are shared by both current stockholders and bondholders. Again, under these circumstances there can be a conflict between stockholders and bondholders with respect to the level of investment.

The Risk-Shifting Problem

Consider a corporation selecting between two mutually exclusive investment projects and financing the chosen project with debt. Both projects require the same investment expenditure and one is riskier than the other in the Rothschild–Stiglitz (1970) sense, i.e., one project has more weight in the tails of its return distribution. Since the investment is made subsequent to obtaining the necessary funds, bondholders do not observe the project choice. Under these circumstances a risk shifting problem may exist, since the corporate manager has the ability to devalue a corporate debt issue by selecting the riskier project.

Consider the use of convertibles in resolving a conflict of interest problem. Corporate management can, for example, encounter a conflict of interests' problem in dealing with bondholders. Since the corporate manager represents the interests of stockholders and bondholders, there is a potential for conflict between the manager and bondholders, or equivalently, between the manager and the bondholders' trustee. This will be the case if it is possible for the manager to take actions that benefit one group and are detrimental to the other. If the bonds represent secured debt then there is no conflict. If not, then an agency problem may exist.

The agency relationship can be thought of as a contract between the principal (i.e., the bondholders' trustee)[1] and an agent (i.e., the corporate manager). The agent acts on behalf of the principal. The contract specifies the bounds on the actions that may be taken by the agent. If the contract covers all possible contingencies then there is no real delegation of authority and so no agency problem. If the contract is incomplete so that the agent has some discretion in the selection of actions then there is at least the potential for a conflict of interests. The conflict occurs because both the principal and the agent behave in accordance with their own self interests. The principal can limit the divergence of interests by providing provisions in the contract that give the agent the appropriate incentives to act in the principal's interest; in addition, the principal can monitor the activity of the agent. It is not usually possible, however, to specify the contract in a way that completely eliminates the conflict of interests' problem. Hence, it may be the case that there is a difference between the action taken by the agent and the action that is in

[1]The legal trustee for the bondholders may be treated as the single principal. It should be added that the trustee acts on behalf of the bondholders. The trustee's problem is the selection of bond covenants that limit the divergence of interests between corporate management and the bondholders. In general, the trustee may have a problem in selecting covenants that provide a solution to the conflict because of the different risk aversion measures of the bondholders. In the case considered here, however, the bondholders will unanimously support a covenant that provides management with the incentive to maximize the risk adjusted net present value of the corporation. It should also be noted that in general there may be an agency problem between the trustee and bondholders (i.e., between the agent and the principals). In the case considered here that problem does not arise because of the unanimity.

the best interests of the principal. The agency cost is defined, by Jensen and Meckling (1976), as the sum of the monitoring expenditures of the principal, the bonding expenditures of the agent, and the residual loss; this residual loss is the loss in the market value of the corporation.[2]

The agency problem we consider here is encountered by the corporation in selecting among mutually exclusive investment projects. Jensen and Smith noted that

> "... the value of the stockholders' equity rises and the value of the bondholders' claim is reduced when the firm substitutes high-risk for low-risk projects."[3]

Of course, bondholders are aware of this possibility, i.e., this attempt to shift risk, and so it is reflected in a lower value for the corporation's debt issue. We want to show that it is possible to construct a convertible bond package that will reduce or eliminate the risk-shifting incentive and so the agency cost of debt. The first step in this process, however, is the demonstration of the agency problem and its cost.

The existence issue

In order to demonstrate the agency problem, suppose the corporation is considering two mutually exclusive investment projects. Call them projects one and two. Let $I_1 = I_2 \equiv I$ denote the dollar cost of the two projects and let Π_1 and Π_2 denote the random project earnings.[4] Suppose project earnings are positive for all states. Suppose project two is riskier than project one, in the Rothschild–Stiglitz sense. In particular, let Π_2 be a mean-preserving spread of Π_1, as shown in Figure 7.1, i.e., $\Pi_2 = (1 + \delta)\Pi_1 - \delta E\Pi_1$,

---

[2]Jensen, M. and W. Meckling (1976). "Theory of the Firm: Managerial Behavior Agency Costs and Ownership Structure." *Journal of Financial Economics* 3: 305–360, also define the residual loss as the dollar equivalent of the loss in expected utility experienced by the principal. Although this notion of residual loss is measurable for a particular principal, this definition poses problems when a trustee represents many principals because the residual loss of any bondholder will depend on the bondholder's measure of risk aversion and on the proportion of the contract owned.

[3]See Jensen, M. and C. Smith (1985). "Stockholder, Manager, and Creditor Interests: Applications of Agency Theory." *Recent Advances in Corporate Finance*. E. Altman and M. Subrahmanyam, eds. Richard D. Irwin. Also see Green, R.C. (1984). "Investment Incentives, Debt, and Warrants." *Journal of Financial Economics* 13: 115–136 and Smith, C. and J. Warner (1979). "On Financial Contracting: An Analysis of Bond Covenants." *Journal of Financial Economics* 7: 117–161, for similar statements.

[4]For notational simplicity, we drop the subscript indicating the corporation and replace it with a subscript indicating the project.

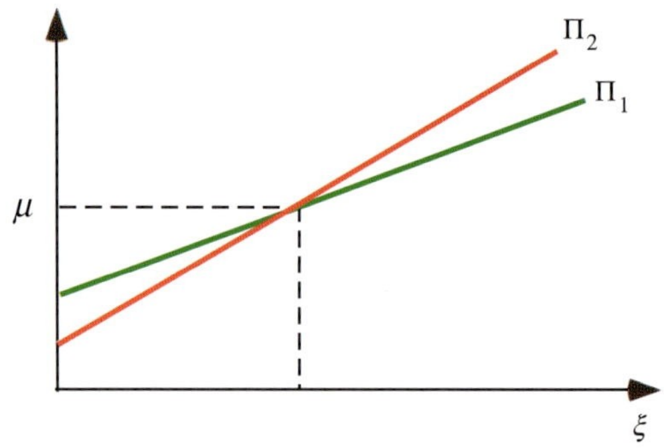

Figure 7.1 Project risk.

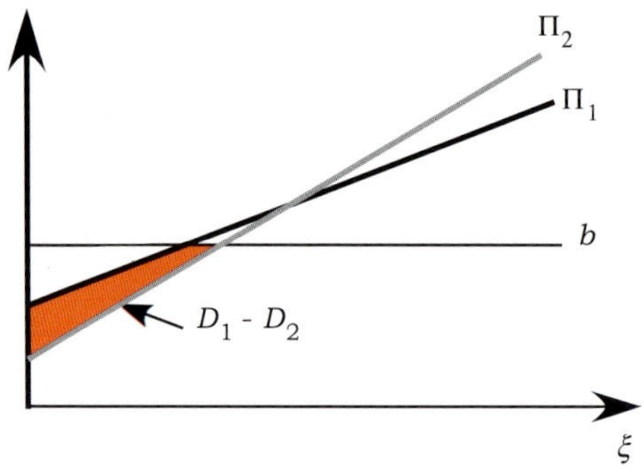

Figure 7.2 Debt devaluation.

$\delta > 0$.[5] Then $\mu_2 = E\Pi_2 = E\Pi_1 = \mu_1$ and Π_2 has more weight in the tails of its distribution, as may be seen in Figure 7.1.

In this context, consider the statement by Jensen and Smith. Suppose bondholders believe that the firm will select project one and value the bond issue accordingly. This means, of course, that the promised payment b on the debt is selected so that the value of the debt issue raises the amount necessary for the investment of I dollars, i.e., $D_1(b) = I$. Next, suppose the firm switches to project two and note that $D_2(b) < D_1(b)$, or equivalently, investors would not have provided the funds necessary for the investment had they known that project two would be selected. If the firm switches then the value of the bondholders' claim is reduced by the amount $D_1 - D_2$, as shown in Figure 7.2.

[5]The state space is still assumed to be finite but it is easier to see the mean-preserving spread when Π is drawn as a continuous function of ω.

Hence, there are circumstances under which it is not rational for the bondholders to believe any claim made by the firm that project one will be selected. Rational bondholders will protect their interests by considering what project will be selected by a management that acts in the best interests of its shareholders.

The first claim we want to make is that there exists a promised payment level b^* such that $S_2(b) > S_1(b)$ for $b > b^*$ and $S_2(b) < S_1(b)$ for $b < b^*$. This may be done simply by showing that in the unlevered case $S_1(0) = V_1 > V_2 = S_2(0)$ and in the sufficiently highly levered case $S_2(b) > S_1(b)$. Then the Intermediate Value Theorem yields the existence of *a* b^*.

Following the outlined procedure, first, we want to show that if the corporation is unlevered and if project two is riskier than project one, then $S_1(0) = V_1 > V_2 = S_2(0)$. Note that the difference in value is

$$\begin{aligned}
V_1 - V_2 &= \int_\Xi \Pi_1(\xi)\,dP - \int_\Xi \Pi_2(\xi)\,dP \\
&= \int_\Xi (\Pi_1(\xi) - \Pi_2(\xi))\,dP \\
&= \delta \int_\Xi (\mu - \Pi_1(\xi))\,dP \\
&= \delta(p\mu - V_1) \\
&> 0
\end{aligned} \tag{7.1}$$

where p is the sum of the basis stock prices. The inequality follows since $p\mu_1 > V_1$, i.e., the present value of a safe asset with the same expected payoff as the project is greater than the risk adjusted present value of the project.[6]

Second, we want to show that in the highly levered case the stock market value of the riskier project is greater. To do this, simply note that for b sufficiently large $\max\{0, \Pi_2 - b\} \geq \max\{0, \Pi_1 - b\}$ for all $\xi \in \Xi$ and strictly greater for some ξ, as shown in Figure 7.3. It follows trivially that

$$\begin{aligned}
S_2(b) &= \int_\Xi \max\{0, \Pi_2(\xi) - b\}\,dP \\
&> \int_\Xi \max\{0, \Pi_1(\xi) - b\}\,dP \\
&= S_1(b)
\end{aligned} \tag{7.2}$$

Then continuity completes the proof and we have the existence of a promised payment level b^* such that $S_2(b) > S_1(b)$ for $b > b^*$ and $S_2(b) < S_1(b)$ for

[6] See MacMinn, R.D. (1987). "Lecture Notes on the Risk-Shifting Problem" for a demonstration of this result.

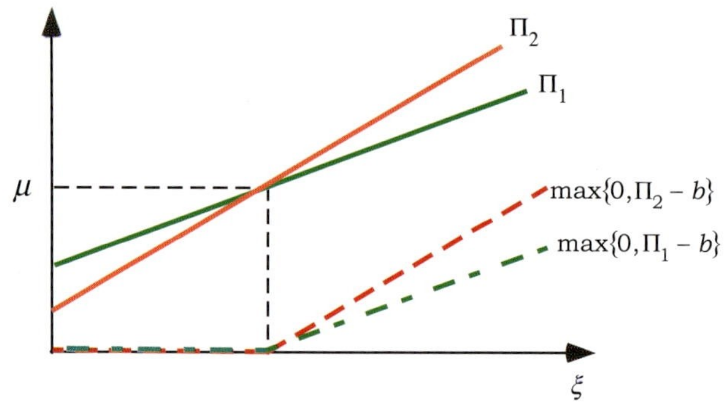

Figure 7.3 Levered stock payoffs.

$b < b^*$. Therefore, in the absence of any mechanism to avoid the agency problem, the corporation with a promised payment $b > b^*$ has an incentive to accept the riskier project.

The agency cost

In its simplest form the agency cost of debt is

$$V_1 - V_2 = \int_{\Xi} (\Pi_1 - \Pi_2)\, dP > 0 \tag{7.3}$$

when the agency problem exists. Actually, claiming that the corporation has an incentive to accept the riskier project is deceptive. Suppose the corporation must make a promised repayment of b_1 dollars in order to finance project one, i.e., $D_1(b_1) = I$, given that bondholders believe that project one will be selected. However, if $b_1 > b^*$ then the corporate management has a moral hazard problem since $S_2(b_1) > S_1(b_1)$. Rational bondholders understand this conflict of interest problem and will value the bond issue as if project two will be selected. Since $D_2(b_1) < I$, it follows that the promised repayment must be increased to $b_2 > b_1$ so that $D_2(b_2) = I$. The equity is appropriately priced as $S_2(b_2)$ but the agency cost is not directly reflected in this expression. It is possible to rewrite the stock market value $S_2(b_2)$ to reflect the agency cost. To do this, note that the promised payment b_2 must be selected so that

$$S_2(b_1) - S_2(b_2) = D_1(b_1) - D_2(b_1)^7 \tag{7.4}$$

[7]This is equivalent to $S_2(b_1) = S_2(b_2) + D_1(b_1) - D_2(b_1)$ which simply says that if the bondholders believe that the firm will select project one and the firm selects project two, then the stock market value of project two is its true value plus the devaluation of the bond issue.

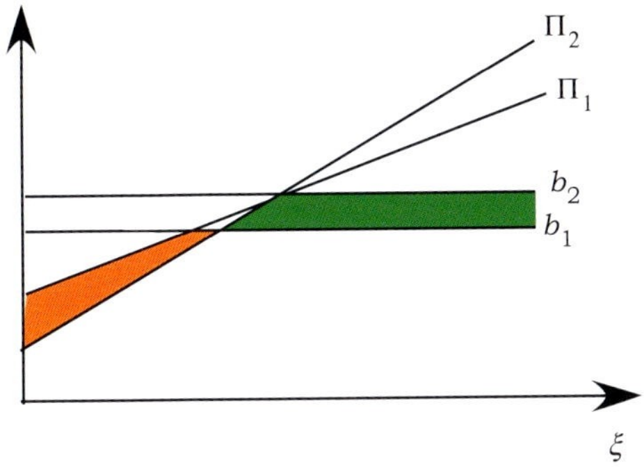

Figure 7.4 Difference in promised payment.

These differences in value are shown in Figure 7.4. Note that $S_2(b_2)$ may be equivalently expressed as

$$S_2(b_2) = S_2(b_1) - (D_1(b_1) - D_2(b_1)) \tag{7.5}$$

Also note that

$$V_1 - V_2 = D_1(b_1) - D_2(b_1) + S_1(b_1) - S_2(b_1)^8 \tag{7.6}$$

or equivalently,

$$S_2(b_1) = S_1(b_1) + (D_1(b_1) - D_2(b_1)) - (V_1 - V_2) \tag{7.7}$$

Then substituting (7.5) into (7.7) and simplifying yields

$$S_2(b_2) = S_1(b_1) - (V_1 - V_2) \tag{7.8}$$

Hence, the stock market value of project two equals that of project one minus the agency cost of the bond issue. Observe that $S_2(b_2) < S_1(b_1)$. This makes it clear that it would be in the best interests of management to convince bondholders that project one will be selected. Because of the moral hazard problem, however, the straight bond contract cannot be used to convince them. With a straight bond contract, the bondholders must expect the devaluation. What is more, at $b_2, S_2(b_2) > S_1(b_2)$ and the higher promised repayment locks management into the choice of project two.

[8]This follows by the 1958 Modigliani–Miller Theorem.

The convertible bond solution

Next, consider the value of convertible bonds. Suppose each bond is issued with a call option which gives its owner the right to exchange a bond for $\theta = \gamma(N+n)/b$ shares of stock, where n is the number of new shares which must be issued if the bonds are converted. Note that a convertible bond is simply a bond with an attached call option. Also note that γ is the fraction of the firm's equity payoff that goes to bondholders in the event that the option is exercised. As has been shown, the payoff on the convertible bond issue is $\min\{\Pi, b\} + \max\{0, \gamma\Pi - b\}$, where b is the exercise value of the call option issue. Then it follows easily that the market value of the convertible bond issue is

$$\begin{aligned} D(b,\gamma) &= \int_{\Xi} \min\{\Pi, b\}\, dP + \int_{\Xi} \max\{0, \gamma\Pi - b\}\, dP \\ &= D(b) + C(b,\gamma) \end{aligned} \tag{7.9}$$

Similarly, the value of the stock is

$$\begin{aligned} S(b,\gamma) &= \int_{\Xi} \max\{0, \Pi - b\}\, dP - \int_{\Xi} \max\{0, \gamma\Pi - b\}\, dP \\ &= \int_{\Xi\setminus B} (\Pi - b)\, dP - \int_{E} (\gamma\Pi - b)\, dP \\ &= S(b) - C(b,\gamma) \end{aligned} \tag{7.10}$$

i.e., the stock market value of the firm with convertible debt is equivalent to the stock market value of the firm with the simple debt contract minus the value of the option. In the second expression for stock value, B is the bankruptcy event and E is the exercise event. Note that the bankruptcy event is $B = \{\xi \in \Xi | \Pi(\xi) < b\} = [0, \delta)$ and the exercise event is $E = \{\xi \in \Xi | \gamma\Pi(\xi) \geq b\} = [\zeta, \omega]$, where $\Xi = [0, \omega]$, as shown in Figure 7.5.

It may be noted that since the corporate value is not affected by the introduction of an option to convert, it follows that the option reduces the stock market value.

Now, consider how management can construct a convertible issue that will convince the bondholders that project one will be selected. In fact, suppose management constructs the package to convince bondholders that project one will be selected and to maximize the stock market value of the corporation by eliminating the agency cost of the bond issue. Suppose management selects the provisions of the bond issue, i.e., (b, γ), so that the project is financed and so that $C_2 - C_1 > D_1 - D_2$. The latter is simply the condition that the difference in the value of the call options exceed the difference in

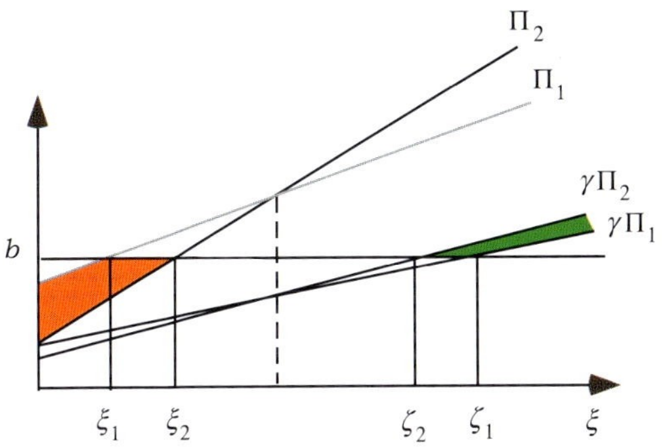

Figure 7.5 The trade-off in values.

the value of the straight bond issues. If bondholders believe that the firm will select project one and so value the bonds accordingly, then by switching to project two the firm can capture the amount $D_1 - D_2$. Equivalently, $D_1 - D_2$ represents the devaluation of the debt claim. $D_1 - D_2$ is represented by the red area in Figure 7.5. Similarly, if project two is selected, given that bondholders believe project one will be selected, then $C_2 - C_1$ represents the increased value of the bondholders' options. The net transfer of wealth to bondholders is $C_2 - C_1 - (D_1 - D_2)$. Note that

$$C_2 - C_1 > D_1 - D_2 \tag{7.11}$$

or equivalently

$$D_2(b) + C_2(b, \gamma) > D_1(b) + C_1(b, \gamma) \tag{7.12}$$

or

$$-D_2(b, \gamma) < -D_1(b, \gamma) \tag{7.13}$$

or

$$V_2 - D_2(b, \gamma) < V_2 - D_1(b, \gamma) < V_1 - D_1(b, \gamma) \tag{7.14}$$

or finally

$$S_2(b, \gamma) < S_1(b, \gamma) \tag{7.15}$$

Hence, any feasible convertible contract which satisfies the condition $C_2 - C_1 > D_1 - D_2$ will convince bondholders that firm management will select project one since that stock value is greater.

It only remains to be shown that this technique of issuing convertible bonds to address the agency problem eliminates the problem and the cost. Recall that $S_2(b_2) = S_1(b_1) - (V_1 - V_2)$. By the 1958 Modigliani–Miller Theorem and the financing conditions, $S_1(b, \gamma) = S_1(b_1)$. It follows that $S_1(b, \gamma) - S_2(b_2) = V_1 - V_2 > 0$. Therefore, the agency cost is eliminated and the manager prefers the convertible debt issue to a straight debt issue.

The solution set

It is possible to solve the risk-shifting problem with a convertible bond issue but how many convertible bond contracts solve the problem and finance the investment? The set of feasible contracts is shown in Figure 7.6. The set of feasible contract is, of course, the set of convertible bonds that finances the investment. The solution set is a subset of this space and the solution set satisfies the following two conditions: (i) $D_1(b, \gamma) = I$; (ii) $D_2(b, \gamma) > D_1(b, \gamma)$. The first condition is the financing condition while the second condition is equivalent to the condition that stock value is greater given the selection of project one.

The conditions implicitly define functional relationships between the contract parameters. The financing constraint yields a function $\gamma = h(b)$; the (b, γ) pairs on h satisfy the financing condition. It may be noted that h is a decreasing function since a larger promised payment on the bond allows a smaller promised equity stake in the event that the bond is converted. To demonstrate this relationship, observe that

$$h' = -\frac{\frac{\partial D_1}{\partial b}}{\frac{\partial D_1}{\partial \gamma}} \leq 0 \tag{7.16}$$

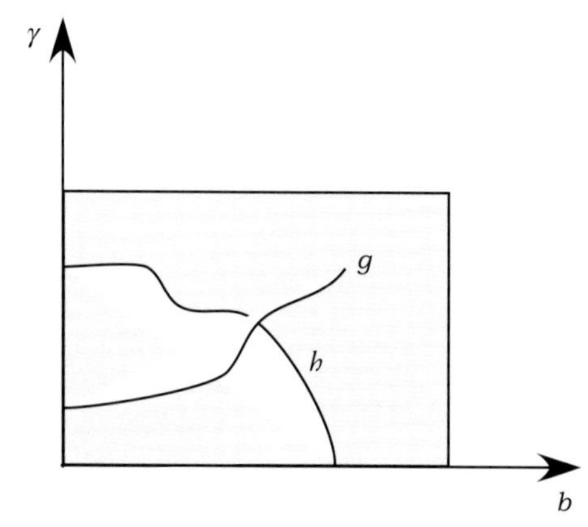

Figure 7.6 The solution set.

since the bond value is increasing in both parameter values, i.e.,

$$\frac{\partial D_1}{\partial b} = \int_{\delta_1}^{\zeta_1} dP \geq 0 \quad \text{and} \quad \frac{\partial D_1}{\partial \gamma} = \int_{\zeta_1}^{x} \Pi_1 dP \geq 0 \tag{7.17}$$

Next, consider the set of parameters (b, γ) such that the convertible bond values are equal, i.e., $D_1(b, \gamma) = D_2(b, \gamma)$; suppose this equality implicitly specifies the function $\gamma = g(b)$. Then

$$g' = -\frac{\frac{\partial D_1}{\partial b} - \frac{\partial D_2}{\partial b}}{\frac{\partial D_1}{\partial \gamma} - \frac{\partial D_2}{\partial \gamma}} > 0 \tag{7.18}$$

since we may observe that

$$\begin{aligned} \frac{\partial D_1}{\partial b} - \frac{\partial D_2}{\partial b} &= \int_{\delta_1}^{\zeta_1} dP - \int_{\delta_2}^{\zeta_2} dP \\ &= \int_{\delta_1}^{\delta_2} dP + \int_{\zeta_2}^{\zeta_1} dP \\ &> 0 \end{aligned} \tag{7.19}$$

and

$$\begin{aligned} \frac{\partial D_1}{\partial \gamma} - \frac{\partial D_2}{\partial \gamma} &= \int_{\zeta_1}^{\omega} \Pi_1 dP - \int_{\zeta_2}^{\omega} \Pi_2 dP \\ &= -\int_{\zeta_2}^{\zeta_1} \Pi_2 dP - \int_{\zeta_1}^{\omega} (\Pi_2 - \Pi_1)\, dP \\ &< 0 \end{aligned} \tag{7.20}$$

The solution set consists of all the contracts (b, γ) on h above g.

The Under-investment Problem

The second of two classic agency problems considered here is the under-investment problem. Notice that acting in the interests of the old shareholders generates the under-investment problem. This problem has been described as limiting the investment expenditure because the additional returns accrue to bondholders as well as stockholders. This problem can be associated with at least two possible scenarios. First, if the firm is already levered enough to make the probability of insolvency positive then the under-investment problem can occur; second, if information concerning the corporate investment opportunity is hidden then the problem can also occur. The first scenario will be considered here briefly and the second will be considered in more detail in the next chapter.

The corporate manager, acting in the interests of the old shareholders, may not invest in positive net present value projects or may under-invest in the projects. This problem occurs because the returns accrue in part to existing bondholders as well as to stockholders. Jensen and Smith observed that

> "... when a substantial portion of the value of the firm is composed of future investment opportunities, a firm with outstanding risky bonds can have incentives to reject positive net present value projects if the benefit from accepting the project accrues to the bondholders."[9]

The incentive need not be so extreme as to cause the manager to reject a project; the manager may under-invest by limiting the size of the project. We will identify the problem in a somewhat general setting without yet attempting to form a solution. One solution to the under-investment problem does exist in the literature, e.g., see Mayers and Smith (1987) and Garven and MacMinn (1993). The solution is provided in an insurance model and there it alters incentives by bundling insurance with a bond contract or equivalently attaching a covenant to the bond instrument that requires insurance and ensures that the net present value of the investment goes to shareholders.

The existence issue

To demonstrate the existence of the problem, suppose the corporate payoff *then* is $\Pi(I,\xi)$[10] and that the firm has previously issued zero coupon bonds with a promised payment of b^o dollars and is now going to make a promised payment of b^n dollars to raise I dollars for an additional project. Suppose that the probability of insolvency is positive, i.e., $P\{\Pi(0,\xi) < b^o\} > 0$. Also suppose that the investment increases the corporate payoff so that

$$\frac{\partial \Pi}{\partial I} > 0 \quad \text{and} \quad \frac{\partial^2 \Pi}{\partial I^2} < 0 \quad \text{for all } \xi \in \Xi \tag{7.21}$$

Suppose that the firm issues new debt with a promised payment b^n to finance the investment of I dollars *now*; finally suppose for simplicity that the new debt is subordinate to the old. The manager paid in salary and corporate

[9]See Jensen, M. and C. Smith (1985). "Stockholder, Manager, and Creditor Interests: Applications of Agency Theory". *Recent Advances in Corporate Finance*. E. Altman and M. Subrahmanyam, eds. Richard D. Irwin, Bodie, Z. and R. Taggart (1978). "Future Investment Opportunities and the Value of the Call Provision on a Bond." *Journal of Finance* 33: 1187–1200, Myers, S. C. (1977). "The Determinants of Corporate Borrowing." *Journal of Financial Economics* 5: 147–175. Smith, C. and J. Warner (1979). "On Financial Contracting: An Analysis of Bond Covenants." *Journal of Financial Economics* 7: 117–161.

[10]The payoff could have been divided into a payoff for previous investments and another for the current investment but that would complicate the notation without adding insight.

stock will make decisions to solve the following constrained maximization problem:

$$\begin{aligned}&\text{maximize } S^o(I)\\&\text{subject to } D^n(b^n) = I\end{aligned} \tag{7.22}$$

where, letting δ be implicitly defined by $\Pi(I,\delta) - b^o - b^n = 0$,

$$\begin{aligned}S^o(I) &= \int_{\Xi} \max\{0, \Pi(I,\xi) - b^o - b^n\}\, dP\\&= \int_{\delta}^{\omega} \left(\Pi(I,\xi) - b^o - b^n\right) dP\end{aligned} \tag{7.23}$$

and, letting δ^o define the boundary of the insolvency event given no new investment,

$$\begin{aligned}D^n(b^n) &= \int_{\Xi} \min\{\max\{0, \Pi(I,\xi) - b^o\}, b^n\}\, dP\\&= \int_{0}^{\delta} \max\{0, \Pi(I,\xi) - b^o\}\, dP + \int_{\delta}^{\omega} b^n dP\\&= \int_{\delta^o}^{\delta} \left(\Pi(I,\xi) - b^o\right) dP + \int_{\delta}^{\omega} b^n dP\end{aligned} \tag{7.24}$$

Let $b^n(I)$ be the required promised payment on new debt required to satisfy the financing condition $D^n(b^n) = I$. Note that

$$\frac{db^n}{dI} = \frac{1}{\int_{\delta}^{\omega} dP}\,^{11} \tag{7.25}$$

Now the unconstrained maximization problem for the firm with debt overhang is

$$\text{maximize } S^o(I) \tag{7.26}$$

where

$$S^o(I) = \int_{\delta}^{\omega} \left(\Pi(I,\xi) - b^o - b^n(I)\right) dP \tag{7.27}$$

---

[11]Observe that

$$\frac{\partial D^n}{\partial b^n} = \left(\Pi(I,\delta) - b^o\right) p(\delta)\frac{\partial \delta}{\partial b^n} + \int_{\delta}^{\omega} dP - b^n p(\delta)\frac{\partial \delta}{\partial b^n} = \int_{\delta}^{\omega} dP$$

and so

$$\frac{db^n}{dI} = \frac{1}{\frac{\partial D^n}{\partial b^n}} = \frac{1}{\int_{\delta}^{\omega} dP}.$$

and the first order condition is

$$\begin{aligned}\frac{dS^o}{dI} &= \int_\delta^\omega \left(D_1\Pi(I,\xi) - \frac{db^n}{dI} \right) dP \\ &= \int_\delta^\omega D_1\Pi(I,\xi)\, dP - \frac{db^n}{dI} \int_\delta^\omega dP \\ &= \int_\delta^\omega D_1\Pi(I,\xi)\, dP - 1 \\ &= 0\end{aligned} \tag{7.28}$$

where the third equality in (7.28) follows by (7.25), or equivalently,

$$\int_\delta^\omega D_1\Pi(I,\xi)\, dP = 1 \tag{7.29}$$

The left hand side of (7.29) is the marginal benefit of the investment for the shareholders while the right hand side is the marginal cost. If there is no positive probability of insolvency then the condition becomes

$$\int_0^\omega D_1\Pi(I,\xi)\, dP = 1 \tag{7.30}$$

If we let I^v satisfy (7.30) and I^s satisfy (7.29) in the debt over-hang case, it is apparent that we have $I^s < I^v$ or equivalently the under-investment problem exists.

Remarks

The risk-shifting and under-investment problems are quite well known in finance. The risk-shifting problem has received a lot of attention and there are well known and costless solutions, e.g., see Green (1984), and MacMinn (1987, 1993). The under-investment problem takes two forms, i.e., with and without asymmetric information. Debt over-hang yields the under-investment problem with symmetric information and has received less attention than its asymmetric cousin. Indeed there only seems to be one solution to one special case of the debt over-hang version of the under-investment problem, e.g., see Mayers and Smith (1987) and Garven and MacMinn (1993). The second version of the under-investment problem is considered in the next chapter.

Suggested Problems

1. Show how to solve the risk-shifting problem with a bond-warrant package.
2. Design a contracting scheme to solve the debt over-hang version of the under-investment problem.

Chapter 8

Information Problems: Hidden Knowledge

Since investors must sometimes contend with incomplete information, the next logical step in describing financial markets entails the introduction of asymmetric information. Of course, asymmetric information characterized the risk shifting problem describe in the last chapter. The information problem there, however, was due to a hidden action and that action could not only be changed but also rationally predicted by the other parties to the financial transaction. The information problem addressed here can be described as hidden knowledge and by that we mean that some market agents possess knowledge about the quality of an asset or project and that quality cannot be altered. Myers and Majluf (1984) considered this hidden knowledge and showed[1] that the hidden knowledge motivates an under-investment problem and can lead to a preference for debt over equity in financing. The latter preference has become known as the pecking order theorem. Like Myers and Majluf, it is supposed here that the information cannot be revealed by the

[1]The Myers–Majluf model is different in some respects. The managers there know the project payoff with certainty and all market agents are risk neutral. While neither assumption is maintained here, the results described by Myers and Majluf are robust to the model here.

choice of the financing scheme.[2] How does the manager who possesses the hidden knowledge make decisions on corporate account? What impact does hidden knowledge have on the choice of investment level and on the capital structure? These questions are addressed here.

If some market participants have access to knowledge that others do not, then it becomes necessary to differentiate between those that do and those that do not have the knowledge. Here we will refer to market agents as insiders and outsiders to describe those who possess and those who do not possess the knowledge, respectively. For simplicity, we suppose that the insiders possess knowledge about the return on their corporation's investment project; that knowledge is hidden from the outsiders. While the corporate management may change the scale of the investment project, the quality of the project is given. The purpose of this chapter is to investigate the implication that the hidden knowledge has for financing and investment decisions in a setting where all market agents, i.e., insiders and outsiders are risk averse and the corporate objective function is endogenously derived.

As in the previous chapters, consider a competitive economy operating between the dates *now* and *then*. All decisions are made *now* and all payoffs on those decisions are received *then*. Here, however, suppose the hidden knowledge exists in one industry where the corporations have either a good or less good investment opportunity. Suppose that trading in financial markets occurs in basis and corporate assets. Finally, suppose that the information possessed by market participants is complete with respect to all the financial markets assets except those of the industry under consideration.

[2]There is also a literature on signaling hidden knowledge and is motivated by the notion that a financial contract can be structured that reveals the hidden knowledge to the market participants. The signaling notion is intriguing but goes beyond the scope of this work; a few examples of that literature are the following: Bhattacharya, S. (1980). "Nondissipative Signaling Structures and Dividend Policy. *Quarterly Journal of Economics* **95**(1): 1–24, Riley, J. G. (1985). "Competition with Hidden Knowledge." *Journal of Political Economy* **93**(5): 958–976, Brennan, M. and A. Kraus (1987). "Efficient Financing under Asymmetric Information." *Journal of Finance* **XLII**(5): 1225–1243, Noe, T. (1988). "Capital Structure and Signaling Game Equilibria." *Review of Financial Studies* **1**: 331–356, Allen, F. and G. R. Faulhaber (1989). "Signaling by Underpricing in the IPO Market." *Journal of Financial Economics* **23**(2): 303–323, Glazer, J. and R. Israel (1990). "Managerial Incentives and Financial Signaling in Product Market Competition." *International Journal of Industrial Organization* 8(2): 271–280, McNichols, M. and A. Dravid (1990). "Stock Dividends, Stock Splits, and Signaling." *Journal of Finance* **45**(3): 857–879, Sobel, J. *et al.* (1990). "Fixed-Equilibrium Rationalizability in Signaling Games." *Journal of Economic Theory* **52**(2): 304–331.

Outsiders

Suppose the financial markets for the assets of corporations in industry F are characterized by hidden knowledge. The knowledge that is hidden specifies the firm's investment opportunity. Suppose there are two types of investment opportunities and so two types of firms in this industry. Let $\Pi_2(\xi) > \Pi_1(\xi)$, for all $\xi \in \Xi$.[3] Firm insiders have complete information, *ex ante*, concerning the corporate payoff functions, individual investors or equivalently outsiders do not. The investor purchasing an asset from a firm in this industry only knows that if state of nature ξ is realized, then the corporate payoff will be $\Pi_1(\xi)$ with probability $1-\theta$ or $\Pi_2(\xi)$ with probability θ; θ is the proportion of firms in the industry that are type two, or equivalently, the probability of randomly selecting a type two firm. Also suppose that the investors know the proportion θ. It follows that the investors know the average industry payoff, i.e., $\Pi_a(\xi) = (1-\theta)\Pi_1(\xi) + \theta\Pi_2(\xi)$.

When an investor purchases an asset from a firm in industry F, the payoff on the asset depends on the state of nature and the firm's type. Since the type is hidden knowledge, it introduces an additional source of risk. The additional risk can be handled in a number of ways. First, although the financial contracts sold by firms in industry F are no longer homogeneous, investors can produce a homogenized asset by purchasing an equal proportion of each firm's assets. Then the payoff on the portfolio is Π_a in each state of nature $\xi \in \Xi$. This eliminates the additional source of risk. In the absence of a screening or signaling mechanism, investors will value firms in this industry on the basis of the average industry payoff and so the value of a firm is V_a, where V_a denotes corporate value from the outsiders' perspective. Consequently, it also follows that the type one firms are over-valued and the type two firms are under-valued in a pooling equilibrium.

Unlevered case

If the corporations in the industry are unlevered then Figure 8.1 shows the corporate value. The stock market value from the outsider's perspective is

$$\begin{aligned} S_a &= \int_\Xi \Pi_a(\xi)\,dP \\ &= \int_\Xi ((1-\theta)\Pi_1(\xi) + \theta\Pi_2(\xi))\,dP \\ &= (1-\theta)\,S_1 + \theta\,S_2 \end{aligned} \tag{8.1}$$

[3]The terms type two and one are used synonymously with high and low investment opportunity, respectively. The inequality conditions guarantee that the random payoff of the high quality firm stochastically dominates that of the low quality firm in the first order sense.

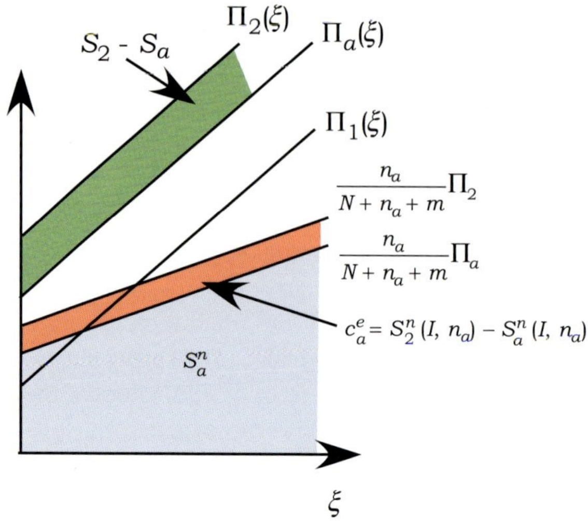

Figure 8.1 Outsiders and value.

Suppose that the unlevered firm has previously issued N shares to the public and m shares to the manager. In addition, the firm issues n_a shares *now* to finance an investment of I dollars. n_a represents the number of shares that must be issued in the presence of the hidden knowledge and will exceed the number n_2 that would have to be issued for the same investment in the absence of the hidden knowledge. The stock market value of the new issue of stock from the insiders' perspective is $S_2^n(I, n_a)$ while it is $S_a^n(I, n_a)$ from the hedged outsiders' perspective. There is some dilution in the value of the current shareholders' stake in the type two corporations as represented by the red area in Figure 8.1. The agency cost of the new equity issue by type two corporations may be characterized as c_a^e where

$$
\begin{aligned}
c_a^e &= S_2^n(I,\, n_a) - S_a^n(I, n_a) \\
&= \frac{n_a}{N + n_a + m}(S_2 - S_a) \qquad (8.2) \\
&> 0
\end{aligned}
$$

The agency cost due to the hidden knowledge is the red area depicted in Figure 8.1; it is also a fraction of the under-valuation of the type two firm and depicted as the green area in Figure 8.1.

Levered case

The capital structure of type two firms determines how the under-valuation is distributed across its assets. Consider a zero coupon bond issue with a promised payment *then* of b dollars. Let D_2 and D_a represent the bond value from the perspective of insiders and outsiders, respectively. Let δ_1 and δ_2 denote the boundaries of the solvency events for the type one and two levered firms respectively. The fully hedged payoff to a risky bond issue by a type two corporation is

$$\begin{cases} \theta\Pi_2 + (1-\theta)\Pi_1 & \text{if } \xi \leq \delta_2 \\ \theta b + (1-\theta)\Pi_1 & \text{if } \delta_2 < \xi < \delta_1 \\ b & \text{if } \xi \geq \delta_1 \end{cases}$$

and so the bond value from the outsiders' perspective is D_a where

$$D_a = \int_0^{\delta_2} \Pi_a \, dP + \int_{\delta_2}^{\delta_1} [\theta b + (1-\theta)\Pi_1] \, dP + \int_{\delta_1}^{\omega} b \, dP \tag{8.3}$$

Since the levered value given the hidden knowledge is

$$D_2 = \int_0^{\delta_2} \Pi_2 \, dP + \int_{\delta_2}^{\omega} b \, dP \tag{8.4}$$

it follows that the extent of the under-valuation of a type two firm's debt is

$$D_2 - D_a = \int_0^{\delta_2} (\Pi_2 - \Pi_a) \, dP + \int_{\delta_2}^{\delta_1} \left[b - (\theta b + (1-\theta)\Pi_1)\right] \, dP \tag{8.5}$$

This is also the agency cost of the debt issue, i.e., $c_a^d = D_2 - D_a$ shown in Figure 8.2.

Similarly, let S_2 and S_a represent the stock market value of a type two firm from the perspective of insiders and outsiders, respectively. The payoff of fully hedged stockholders is

$$\begin{cases} 0 & \text{if } \xi \leq \delta_2 \\ \theta(\Pi_2 - b) & \text{if } \delta_2 < \xi < \delta_1 \\ \Pi_a - b & \text{if } \xi \geq \delta_1 \end{cases}$$

The outsider stock value is S_a where

$$S_a = \int_{\delta_2}^{\delta_1} \theta(\Pi_2 - b) \, dP + \int_{\delta_1}^{\omega} (\Pi_a - b) \, dP \tag{8.6}$$

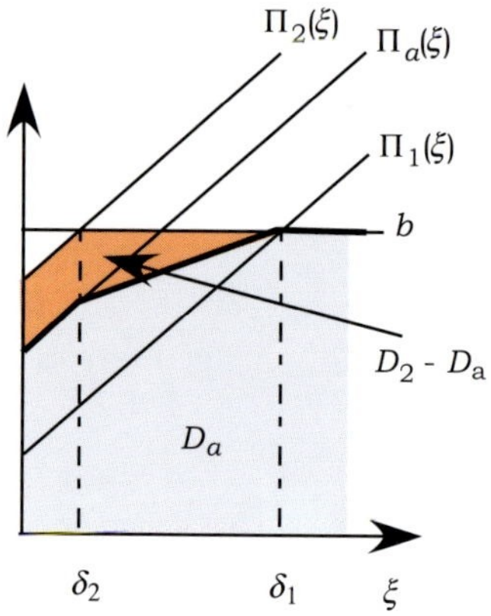

Figure 8.2 Hidden knowledge and the agency cost of debt.

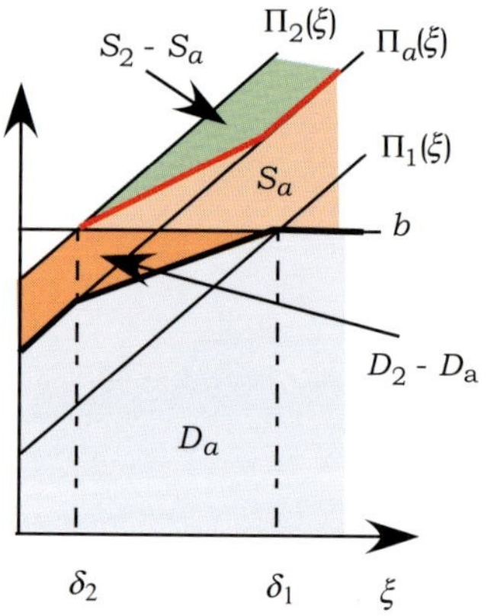

Figure 8.3 Hidden knowledge and levered values.

The outsider equity value is shown in Figure 8.3. Then, the extent of the under-valuation of a type two firm's equity is

$$S_2 - S_a = \int_{\delta_2}^{\delta_1} (1 - \theta)(\Pi_2 - b)\, dP + \int_{\delta_1}^{\omega} (\Pi_2 - \Pi_a)\, dP \geq 0$$

These results present corporate management with adverse incentives. The adverse incentives become evident once the corporate manager's objective function is identified. If the manager cannot trade on the hidden knowledge then the self interested corporate manager will make investment and financing decisions to maximize her own stake in the corporation. The manager makes decisions to maximize S_2^o and that current shareholder value can also be represented as $V_2 - I - c_a$, where V_2 is the corporate value of the high quality firm given insider information, I is the dollar amount raised from outsiders, and c_a is the agency cost of outside finance.[4] Hence, as Myers and Majluf noted, there are circumstances under which the firm will reject positive net present value projects, i.e., if $V_2 - I < c_a$.[5] More generally, the firm may simply invest less than the amount that maximizes the risk adjusted net present value of the corporation. This is one form that the adverse selection problem can take. Even if the adverse selection problem is not severe enough to cause the firm to reject the project, i.e., $V_2 - I > c_a$, the hidden knowledge still has an impact because the manager selects the financing method which minimizes the agency cost. This contract selection is important because, if the high quality firm cannot provide outsiders with credible information about its quality, then the appropriate selection of a contract is the only means the firm has available to mitigate the effects of the adverse selection problem.

Insiders

The hidden knowledge yields an adverse selection problem for corporate managers in the industry. The hidden knowledge generally makes it more costly for the type two firms to issue some financial contracts. The kind of financial instrument the firm chooses to issue becomes relevant in this setting because not all instruments yield the same agency cost. For example, Myers and Majluf demonstrated that a safe debt issue eliminates the agency cost of outside finance and so is preferred to an equity issue. This hidden knowledge also affects the manager's behavior on personal account because the type two managers cannot borrow against the full value of her equity stake in the corporation. This manager also knows that there will be a capital gain when the hidden knowledge becomes public and so the information affects the portfolio decision, e.g., fewer basis assets need to be purchased for those states in which the manager knows there will be a capital gain. It is assumed here that the manager cannot trade on inside information and that the manager's portfolio decision is a hidden action. Both types of decisions on personal account

[4] See the analysis in the next section to confirm these claims.

[5] There are significant differences between this model and that of Myers and Majluf but some of their conclusions are sufficiently robust to apply in the context of this model. Unlike this model, Myers and Majluf did not allow for risk aversion and the corporate manager was assumed to know which of two states of nature would occur then.

$$\begin{aligned}\frac{\partial L}{\partial I} &= \int_{\Xi} D_2 u\left(\frac{m}{N+n_a+m}\frac{\partial g}{\partial I}\right) d\Psi \\ &\quad +\lambda\left(\frac{m}{N+n+m}\frac{\partial S_a}{\partial I}\right)+\eta\left(\frac{n}{N+n+m}\frac{\partial S_a}{\partial I}-1\right) \\ &= 0\end{aligned} \tag{8.12}$$

$$\begin{aligned}\frac{\partial L}{\partial n} &= \int_{\Xi} D_2 u\left(-\frac{m}{(N+n+m)^2}g(I,\xi)\right) d\Psi \\ &\quad -\lambda\left(\frac{m}{(N+n+m)^2}S_a(I)\right)+\eta\left(\frac{(N+n+m)-n}{(N+n+m)^2}S_a(I)\right) \\ &= 0\end{aligned} \tag{8.13}$$

$$\frac{\partial L}{\partial \lambda} = -\left(c_0 + \int_{\Xi} c_1(\xi)\, dP - \left(m_0 + \int_{\Xi} m_1(\xi)\, dP + \frac{m}{N+n+m}S_a(I)\right)\right) = 0 \tag{8.14}$$

$$\frac{\partial L}{\partial \eta} = S_a^n(I) - I = 0 \tag{8.15}$$

Observe that

$$\frac{\partial g}{\partial I} = \frac{\partial \Pi_2}{\partial I} - \frac{\partial \Pi_a}{\partial I} = (1-\theta)\frac{\partial \Pi_2}{\partial I} \tag{8.16}$$

It follows that (8.12) may be equivalently expressed as

$$\begin{aligned}\frac{\partial L}{\partial I} &= \int_{\Xi} D_2 u\left(\frac{m}{N+n_a+m}(1-\theta)\frac{\partial \Pi_2}{\partial I}\right) d\Psi \\ &\quad +\lambda\left(\frac{m}{N+n+M}\frac{\partial S_a}{\partial I}\right)+\eta\left(\frac{n}{N+n+m}\frac{\partial S_a}{\partial I}-1\right) \\ &= 0\end{aligned} \tag{8.17}$$

Substituting (8.11) into (8.17) yields

$$\begin{aligned}\frac{\partial L}{\partial I} &= \lambda\int_{\Xi}\left(\frac{m}{N+n+m}(1-\theta)\frac{\partial \Pi_2}{\partial I}\right) dP \\ &\quad +\lambda\left(\frac{m}{N+n+M}\theta\frac{\partial \Pi_2}{\partial I}\right)+\eta\left(\frac{n}{N+n+m}\frac{\partial S_a}{\partial I}-1\right) \\ &= \lambda\int_{\Xi}\left(\frac{m}{N+n+m}\frac{\partial \Pi_2}{\partial I}\right) dP+\eta\left(\frac{n}{N+n+m}\frac{\partial S_a}{\partial I}-1\right) \\ &= \lambda\left(\frac{m}{N+n+m}\frac{\partial S_2}{\partial I}\right)+\eta\left(\frac{n}{N+n+m}\frac{\partial S_a}{\partial I}-1\right) \\ &= 0\end{aligned} \tag{8.18}$$

makes decisions to maximize S_2^o and that current shareholder value can also be represented as $V_2 - I - c_a$, where V_2 is the corporate value of the high quality firm given insider information, I is the dollar amount raised from outsiders, and c_a is the agency cost of outside finance.[4] Hence, as Myers and Majluf noted, there are circumstances under which the firm will reject positive net present value projects, i.e., if $V_2 - I < c_a$.[5] More generally, the firm may simply invest less than the amount that maximizes the risk adjusted net present value of the corporation. This is one form that the adverse selection problem can take. Even if the adverse selection problem is not severe enough to cause the firm to reject the project, i.e., $V_2 - I > c_a$, the hidden knowledge still has an impact because the manager selects the financing method which minimizes the agency cost. This contract selection is important because, if the high quality firm cannot provide outsiders with credible information about its quality, then the appropriate selection of a contract is the only means the firm has available to mitigate the effects of the adverse selection problem.

Insiders

The hidden knowledge yields an adverse selection problem for corporate managers in the industry. The hidden knowledge generally makes it more costly for the type two firms to issue some financial contracts. The kind of financial instrument the firm chooses to issue becomes relevant in this setting because not all instruments yield the same agency cost. For example, Myers and Majluf demonstrated that a safe debt issue eliminates the agency cost of outside finance and so is preferred to an equity issue. This hidden knowledge also affects the manager's behavior on personal account because the type two managers cannot borrow against the full value of her equity stake in the corporation. This manager also knows that there will be a capital gain when the hidden knowledge becomes public and so the information affects the portfolio decision, e.g., fewer basis assets need to be purchased for those states in which the manager knows there will be a capital gain. It is assumed here that the manager cannot trade on inside information and that the manager's portfolio decision is a hidden action. Both types of decisions on personal account

---

[4] See the analysis in the next section to confirm these claims.

[5] There are significant differences between this model and that of Myers and Majluf but some of their conclusions are sufficiently robust to apply in the context of this model. Unlike this model, Myers and Majluf did not allow for risk aversion and the corporate manager was assumed to know which of two states of nature would occur then.

have the potential to reveal information to outsiders.[6] Less than complete revelation of the manager's portfolio decision does not necessarily eliminate the hidden knowledge problem, e.g., a long public position in the stock may be counter-balanced by a short private position.

The existence of hidden knowledge creates some difficulty in identifying optimal decisions not only for type one and two managers but also for bondholders. The revelation of that knowledge is jointly determined by the decisions made by the corporate managers and the bondholders. In the analysis which follows, the objective functions used by type one and two managers for decisions on corporate account are derived. It is assumed throughout this analysis that each manager's compensation is a known salary plus an equity stake in the corporation.[7]

An equity issue

First, consider the manager of a type two firm. The manager makes a portfolio decision on personal account, and investment and financing decisions on corporate account. The purpose of this analysis is to show that the personal and corporate decisions are separable and that the manager has a well-defined objective function for all corporate decisions that does not depend on her measure of risk aversion or probability beliefs. Suppose the type two manager issues equity to finance the corporate investment. The manager has hidden knowledge and an equity stake in the corporation. Suppose that $N + m$ shares have been previously issued, where N represents the number that are publicly held and m represents the number of shares held by the manager. The manager will issue n new shares *now* to finance the investment decision that she makes. The manager knows that there will be a capital gain of g dollars to insiders *then*, where g depends on the terms of the financial package and on the investment decision. In this case of a new stock issue, the capital gain is defined as

$$g(I, \xi) = (\Pi_2(I, \xi) - \Pi_a(I, \xi)) \tag{8.7}$$

The capital gain is not tradable and so it is expressed as part of the consumption *then* term, i.e., $c_1(\xi) + \frac{m}{N+n+m}g$, where $c_1(\xi)$ represents the

[6] Leland and Pyle use the manager's portfolio decision as a signal to outsiders, i.e., see Leland, H. and D. Pyle (1977). "Informational Asymmetries, Financial Structure and Financial Intermediation." *Journal of Finance* 32: 371–387.

[7] A compensation scheme which consists of a salary plus a risky bonus or a risky stock option package would cause a fundamental change in the analysis because of the altered incentive effects. See MacMinn, R. and F. Page (1995). "Stock Options, Managerial Incentives, and Capital Structure." *Journal of Financial Studies* Dec.

net consumption *then*. The common knowledge is represented as the payoff *then* on the equity. The common knowledge component augments the manager's income *then*. The manager can borrow against this value and so it is represented in the budget constraint. The self-interested manager faces the following problem:

$$\begin{aligned}\text{maximize } & \int_{\Xi} u\left(c_0, c_1(\xi) + \frac{m}{N+n+m} g(I,\xi)\right) d\Psi \\ \text{subject to } c_0 + & \int_{\Xi} c_1(\xi)\, dP = m_0 + \int_{\Xi} m_1(\xi)\, dP + \frac{m}{N+n+m} S_a(I) \\ \text{and } \quad & S_a^n(I) = I\end{aligned} \tag{8.8}$$

The first constraint in (8.8) is the budget hyperplane that simply says that the risk adjusted present value of consumption equals the risk adjusted present value of income. The second constraint is the financing condition that implicitly defines the number of new shares that must be issued for each possible investment decision given the common knowledge. The constrained expected utility maximization problem for the type one manager is analogous and so is not stated here. The only difference is that the type one manager's hidden knowledge yields a known capital loss.

The Lagrange function corresponding to (8.8) is

$$\begin{aligned}L(I,n,\lambda,\eta) = & \int_{\Xi} u\left(c_0, c_1(\xi) + \frac{m}{N+n+m} g(I,\xi)\right) d\Psi \\ & - \lambda\left(c_0 + \int_{\Xi} c_1(\xi)\, dP - \left(m_0 + \int_{\Xi} m_1(\xi)\, dP \right.\right. \\ & \left.\left. + \frac{m}{N+n+m} S_a(I)\right)\right) \\ & + \eta\left(S_a^n(I) - I\right)\end{aligned} \tag{8.9}$$

where λ and η are the Lagrange multipliers. The type two manager makes decisions on personal and corporate account to optimize (8.8) or equivalently (8.9) where the stock value $S_a(I)$ is expressed in (8.1), the gain g is expressed in (8.7). Maximizing the Lagrange function yields the following first order conditions for a maximum:

$$\frac{\partial L}{\partial c_0} = \int_{\Xi} D_1 u\, d\Psi - \lambda = 0 \tag{8.10}$$

$$\frac{\partial L}{\partial c_1(\xi)} = D_2 u \psi(\xi) - \lambda p(\xi) = 0, \quad \text{for all } \xi \in \Xi \tag{8.11}$$

$$
\begin{aligned}
\frac{\partial L}{\partial I} &= \int_{\Xi} D_2 u \left(\frac{m}{N + n_a + m} \frac{\partial g}{\partial I} \right) d\Psi \\
&\quad + \lambda \left(\frac{m}{N + n + m} \frac{\partial S_a}{\partial I} \right) + \eta \left(\frac{n}{N + n + m} \frac{\partial S_a}{\partial I} - 1 \right) \\
&= 0
\end{aligned}
\tag{8.12}
$$

$$
\begin{aligned}
\frac{\partial L}{\partial n} &= \int_{\Xi} D_2 u \left(-\frac{m}{(N + n + m)^2} g(I, \xi) \right) d\Psi \\
&\quad - \lambda \left(\frac{m}{(N + n + m)^2} S_a(I) \right) + \eta \left(\frac{(N + n + m) - n}{(N + n + m)^2} S_a(I) \right) \\
&= 0
\end{aligned}
\tag{8.13}
$$

$$
\frac{\partial L}{\partial \lambda} = - \left(c_0 + \int_{\Xi} c_1(\xi)\, dP - \left(m_0 + \int_{\Xi} m_1(\xi)\, dP + \frac{m}{N + n + m} S_a(I) \right) \right) = 0
\tag{8.14}
$$

$$
\frac{\partial L}{\partial \eta} = S_a^n(I) - I = 0
\tag{8.15}
$$

Observe that

$$
\frac{\partial g}{\partial I} = \frac{\partial \Pi_2}{\partial I} - \frac{\partial \Pi_a}{\partial I} = (1 - \theta) \frac{\partial \Pi_2}{\partial I}
\tag{8.16}
$$

It follows that (8.12) may be equivalently expressed as

$$
\begin{aligned}
\frac{\partial L}{\partial I} &= \int_{\Xi} D_2 u \left(\frac{m}{N + n_a + m} (1 - \theta) \frac{\partial \Pi_2}{\partial I} \right) d\Psi \\
&\quad + \lambda \left(\frac{m}{N + n + M} \frac{\partial S_a}{\partial I} \right) + \eta \left(\frac{n}{N + n + m} \frac{\partial S_a}{\partial I} - 1 \right) \\
&= 0
\end{aligned}
\tag{8.17}
$$

Substituting (8.11) into (8.17) yields

$$
\begin{aligned}
\frac{\partial L}{\partial I} &= \lambda \int_{\Xi} \left(\frac{m}{N + n + m} (1 - \theta) \frac{\partial \Pi_2}{\partial I} \right) dP \\
&\quad + \lambda \left(\frac{m}{N + n + M} \theta \frac{\partial \Pi_2}{\partial I} \right) + \eta \left(\frac{n}{N + n + m} \frac{\partial S_a}{\partial I} - 1 \right) \\
&= \lambda \int_{\Xi} \left(\frac{m}{N + n + m} \frac{\partial \Pi_2}{\partial I} \right) dP + \eta \left(\frac{n}{N + n + m} \frac{\partial S_a}{\partial I} - 1 \right) \\
&= \lambda \left(\frac{m}{N + n + m} \frac{\partial S_2}{\partial I} \right) + \eta \left(\frac{n}{N + n + m} \frac{\partial S_a}{\partial I} - 1 \right) \\
&= 0
\end{aligned}
\tag{8.18}
$$

Similarly, substituting from (8.11) and (8.7) into (8.13) yields

$$
\begin{aligned}
\frac{\partial L}{\partial n} &= \lambda \int_{\Xi} \left(-\frac{m}{(N+n+m)^2} (\Pi_2(I,\xi) - \Pi_a(I,\xi)) \right) dP \\
&\quad -\lambda \left(\frac{m}{(N+n+m)^2} S_a(I) \right) + \eta \left(\frac{N+m}{(N+n+m)^2} S_a(I) \right) \\
&= \lambda \frac{-m}{(N+n+m)^2} S_2(I) + \eta \left(\frac{N+m}{(N+n+m)^2} S_a(I) \right) \\
&= 0
\end{aligned}
\tag{8.19}
$$

A few observations are in order now. Note that (8.18), (8.19) and (8.15) correspond to the first order conditions for the solution to the following constrained maximization problem:

$$
\begin{aligned}
&\text{maximize } \frac{m}{N+n+m} S_2(I) \\
&\text{subject to } \frac{n}{N+n+m} S_a(I) = I
\end{aligned}
\tag{8.20}
$$

This makes it apparent[8] that we have a Fisher separation result, since the solution to this problem is independent of the decision maker's intertemporal preferences, measure of risk aversion and probability beliefs. It should be emphasized that $S_2(I)$ is not common knowledge and so the manager makes a decision based on the hidden knowledge. Of course the hidden knowledge yields the dilution in the equity stakes of the current shareholders and that dilution is implicit in the financing constraint in (8.20). The objective function in (8.20) might come as a surprise, since the common assumption in the literature, e.g., see Myers and Majluf (1984), is that the manager makes decisions to maximize the value of the current shareholders' stake in the corporation.

A few questions ought to be addressed at this point. Does the manager make decisions that are in the interests of current shareholders? For this question, note that the manager acting in the interests of current shareholders

[8] To confirm this assertion, let the Lagrange function be $L(I, n, \lambda, \eta) = \lambda\left(\frac{m}{N+n+m} S_2\right) + \eta\left(\frac{n}{N+n+m} S_a - I\right)$ and show the correspondence by direct calculation.

would make the investment decision to solve the following problem:

$$\begin{aligned} &\text{maximize } \frac{N+m}{N+n+m} S_2(I) \\ &\text{subject to } \frac{n}{N+n+m} S_a(I) = I \end{aligned} \tag{8.21}$$

Equivalently if we let $n_a(I)$[9] denote the number of new shares issued to finance the investment decision and state the problem in unconstrained form then it may be expressed as either

$$\text{maximize } \frac{N+m}{N+n_a(I)+m} S_2(I) \tag{8.22}$$

or equivalently as

$$\text{maximize } V_2(I) - I - c_a(I) \tag{8.23}$$

where c_a is the agency cost of the new issue.[10] The agency cost is

$$c_a = \frac{n_a}{N+n_a+m}(S_2 - S_a) > 0 \tag{8.24}$$

Hence, the objective function of the manager here paid in stock is different from that found in the literature and stresses the importance of deriving the objective function rather than assuming it. Of course, in this case we must also note that the manager paid in share here will make investment decision to solve the constrained maximization problem in (8.20) or equivalently the

[9]Observe that this function is implicitly defined by the constraint and direct calculation shows that $n_a(I) = N\frac{I}{S_a(I)-I}$.

[10]This observation follows since

$$\begin{aligned} V_2(I) - I - c_a &= S_2 - I - \frac{n_a}{N+n_a+m} S_2 + S_a^n \\ &= S_2 - \frac{n_a}{N+n_a+m} S_2 \\ &= \frac{N+m}{N+n_a+m} S_2 \end{aligned}$$

unconstrained problem in (8.25)

$$\text{maximize } \frac{m}{N + n_a(I) + m} S_2(I) \tag{8.25}$$

but it may be noted that

$$\begin{aligned} \frac{m}{N + n_a(I) + m} S_2(I) &= \frac{m}{N + m} \left(\frac{N + m}{N + n_a(I) + m} S_2(I) \right) \\ &= \frac{m}{N + m} (S_2(I) - I - c_a(I)) \end{aligned} \tag{8.26}$$

Hence it is clear that despite the somewhat different objective function, the manager will select the investment in the interests of current shareholders.

Another question is whether there an under-investment problem? The fact that there is a positive agency cost c_a makes it apparent that an agency cost exists and affects the decisions made by the manager. Given the expression of the problem in (8.26), it is apparent that an under-investment problem exists if the marginal agency cost is positive. Note that

$$\begin{aligned} c'_a(I) &= \frac{(N + n_a + m)n'_a - n_a n'_a}{(N + n_a + m)^2} (S_2 - S_a) + \frac{n_a}{N + n_a + m} \left(S'_2(I) - S'_a(I) \right) \\ &= \frac{(N + m)n'_a}{(N + n_a + m)^2} (S_2 - S_a) + \frac{n_a}{N + n_a + m} \left(S'_2(I) - S'_a(I) \right) \\ &> 0 \end{aligned} \tag{8.27}$$

since n_a is an increasing function of the investment level and the difference of marginal stock values in the second term is positive. Hence, the manager under-invests.

A debt issue

Next, suppose the manager selects a debt issue to finance the new investment for the firm. Again, consider the manager of a type two firm. The manager makes a portfolio decision on personal account, and investment and financing decisions on corporate account. Suppose the type two manager issues debt to finance the corporate investment. As before, suppose $N + m$ shares have been previously issued, where N represents the number of shares that are publicly held and m represents the number of shares that are held by the manager. The manager knows that there will be a capital gain of g dollars to insiders *then*, where g depends on the terms of the financial package and on the investment decision. In this case of a zero coupon bond issue, the capital gain is defined as

$$\begin{aligned} g(I,b,\xi) &= (\max\{0,\Pi_2(I,\xi)-b\} - \max\{0,\Pi_a(I,\xi)-b\}) \\ &= (\Pi_2(I,\xi) - \Pi_a(I,\xi)) \end{aligned} \tag{8.28}$$

where the second equality holds if and only if the debt issue is safe. The manager's decision on personal and corporate account are made to solve the following problem:

$$\begin{aligned} &\text{maximize} \int_\Xi u\left(c_0, c_1(\xi) + \frac{m}{N+m} g(I,b,\xi)\right) d\Psi \\ &\text{subject to } c_0 + \int_\Xi c_1(\xi)\, dP = m_0 + \int_\Xi m_1(\xi)\, dP + \frac{m}{N+m} S_a(I,b) \\ &\text{and} \quad D_a(I,b) = I \end{aligned} \tag{8.29}$$

where the stock value from the outsider's perspective is given in (8.6) and the bond market value from the outsiders' perspective is given in (8.3).

The Lagrange function corresponding to the constrained maximization problem in (8.29) is

$$\begin{aligned} L(I,b,\lambda,\eta) = &\int_\Xi u\left(c_0, c_1(\xi) + \frac{m}{N+m} g(I,b,\xi)\right) d\Psi \\ &- \lambda\left(c_0 + \int_\Xi c_1(\xi)\, dP - \left(m_0 + \int_\Xi m_1(\xi)\, dP \right.\right. \\ &\left.\left. + \frac{m}{N+m} S_a(I,b)\right)\right) \\ &+ \eta(D_a(I,b) - I) \end{aligned} \tag{8.30}$$

The first order conditions for the decisions on personal account remain the same as those stated in Equations (8.10) and (8.11). The first order conditions for the decisions on corporate account are as follows:

$$\begin{aligned} \frac{\partial L}{\partial I} = &\int_\Xi D_2 u\left(\frac{m}{N+m}\frac{\partial g}{\partial I}\right) d\Psi \\ &+ \lambda\left(\frac{m}{N+m}\frac{\partial S_a}{\partial I}\right) + \eta\left(\frac{\partial D_a}{\partial I} - 1\right) \\ = &\ 0 \end{aligned} \tag{8.31}$$

$$\begin{aligned}\frac{\partial L}{\partial b} &= \int_{\Xi} D_2 u \left(\frac{m}{N+m} \frac{\partial g}{\partial b} \right) d\Psi \\ &\quad + \lambda \left(\frac{m}{N+m} \frac{\partial S_a}{\partial b} \right) + \eta \left(\frac{\partial D_a}{\partial b} \right) \\ &= 0\end{aligned} \tag{8.32}$$

Substituting from (8.11) and (8.28) into (8.31) and (8.32) yields

$$\begin{aligned}\frac{\partial L}{\partial I} &= \lambda \int_{\Xi} \left(\frac{m}{N+m} \frac{\partial g}{\partial I} \right) dP \\ &\quad + \lambda \left(\frac{m}{N+m} \frac{\partial S_a}{\partial I} \right) + \eta \left(\frac{\partial D_a}{\partial I} - 1 \right) \\ &= \lambda \frac{m}{N+m} \left(\frac{\partial S_2}{\partial I} - \frac{\partial S_a}{\partial I} \right) \\ &\quad + \lambda \left(\frac{m}{N+m} \frac{\partial S_a}{\partial I} \right) + \eta \left(\frac{\partial D_a}{\partial I} - 1 \right) \\ &= \lambda \frac{m}{N+m} \frac{\partial S_2}{\partial I} + \eta \left(\frac{\partial D_a}{\partial I} - 1 \right) \\ &= 0\end{aligned} \tag{8.33}$$

and

$$\begin{aligned}\frac{\partial L}{\partial b} &= \lambda \int_{\Xi} \left(\frac{m}{N+m} \frac{\partial g}{\partial b} \right) dP \\ &\quad + \lambda \left(\frac{m}{N+m} \frac{\partial S_a}{\partial b} \right) + \eta \left(\frac{\partial D_a}{\partial b} \right) \\ &= \lambda \frac{m}{N+m} \frac{\partial S_2}{\partial b} + \eta \frac{\partial D_a}{\partial b} \\ &= 0\end{aligned} \tag{8.34}$$

As previously, observe that the first order conditions for the corporate account decisions are equivalent to the first order conditions for the following problem

$$\begin{aligned}&\text{maximize } \frac{m}{N+m} S_2(I, b) \\ &\text{subject to } D_a(I, b) = I\end{aligned} \tag{8.35}$$

Hence, a Fisher separation result has been established in this case as well.

Also, if we let $b_a(I)$ denote the promised payment on debt necessary to finance the investment decision and state the problem in unconstrained form, it may be expressed as either

$$\text{maximize } \frac{m}{N+m} S_2(I, b_a(I)) \tag{8.36}$$

or

$$\text{maximize } \frac{m}{N+m} \left(V_2 - I - c_a^d\right) \tag{8.37}$$

where c_a^d represents the agency cost of the debt issue. The agency cost of the debt issue is

$$c_a^d(I) = D_2(I, b_a(I)) - D_a(I, b_a(I)) \tag{8.38}$$

and is depicted in Figure 8.2. There are several versions of the objective function presented here in the levered case but all show that the manager has the incentive to maximize the current shareholder value.

Finally, consider whether the manager will under-invest due to the hidden knowledge in this levered case. There is a non-negative agency cost c_a^d that makes it apparent that an agency cost exists and affects the decisions made by the manager. Given the expression of the problem in (8.37), it is apparent that an under-investment problem exists if the marginal agency cost is positive.

The Pecking Order

In each statement of the insider's decision problem, it has been apparent that there is a potential for under-investment. There is also a capital structure decision that becomes more important in this setting because, if the under-investment problem can be solved then the associated agency cost can be eliminated and so the current shareholder value increased. The following is a statement of the result reported by Myers and Majluf that has also become known as the pecking order theorem.

1984 Myers–Majluf Theorem. If the firm is endowed with a project that may either be good or bad and the firm insiders know the project type but firm outsiders do not, *ceteris paribus*, the firm may reject the good project if outside equity must be issued to finance it. The current shareholders bear an agency cost due to the asymmetric information if the firm issues equity. If the firm can issue safe debt to finance the good project, then it will not be rejected and the current shareholders will not bear an agency cost.

Figure 8.4 depicts a case in which the type two corporate manager may issue debt that is safe. Type two corporations are under-valued as shown

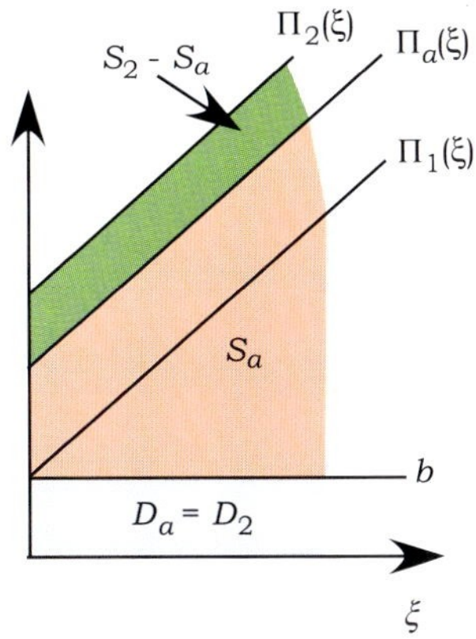

Figure 8.4 The pecking order.

in the figure but those managers trade on personal account knowing the capital gain that they will participate in when the hidden information is revealed *then*. What is more, since debt is used there is no dilution necessary in the current shareholders stake which would otherwise be necessary in an equity issue. The promised repayment on debt for the optimal investment is sufficiently small, so that the debt must be viewed as safe even though outsiders do not know the firm type. Hence while the agency cost of equity would be positive, the agency cost of debt is zero, i.e., $c_a^d = D_2(I, b) - D_a(I, b) = 0$. It follows that the manager will prefer debt to equity as long as the debt issue is safe from the outsiders' perspective. It should also follow that debt is still preferred for sufficiently small promised payments that yield a positive probability of insolvency. What is not apparent, however, is whether debt remains the dominant choice as the leverage increases.

Suggested Problems

1. Suppose firms have earnings *now* that may be used to finance the investment choice. Derive the manager's objective function.
2. How does the introduction of earnings *now* affect the pecking order? Will earnings retained and re-invested be preferred to a safe debt issue, or a risky debt issue?
3. Suppose corporate managers are compensated with stock options rather than stock. Derive the manager's objective function. Will such a manager have a preference for debt over equity? Does the preference extend to risky debt?

Chapter 9

Corporate Risk Management

Risks are commodities that may be exchanged. The corporation, long viewed as a nexus of contracts (Alchian and Demsetz 1972), may also be viewed as a nexus of risks. The corporation may be described as a composite commodity or bundle of risks that may be further aggregated or separated.

> "... the history of the development of risk instruments is a tale of the progressive separation of risks, enabling each to be borne in the least expensive way." (Kohn 1999).

An economy may achieve an efficient allocation of risks as well as resources through separation and trading, i.e., see Arrow (1963) and Debreu (1959). Risk has long been studied but despite the progress and the new perspectives, the notion is still elusive.

Both the 1958 Modigliani–Miller Theorem and the Capital Asset Pricing Model (CAPM) (Sharpe 1964; Mossin 1966) have had an impact on our perception of risk and value. The message of both is that, *ceteris paribus*, hedging does not increase value. An entire literature has been generated since those early contributions that deals with the issue of risk and value. This literature provides a few tentative steps in establishing a positive connection between risk management and value (e.g., Jensen and Meckling 1976; Myers 1977; Mayers and Smith 1982; Main 1983; Green 1984; Myers and Majluf 1984; Stulz 1984; Smith and Stulz 1985; MacMinn 1987; MacMinn 1987; Mayers and Smith 1987; Froot *et al.* 1993; Garven and MacMinn 1993; Froot *et al.* 1994). The motivations for risk management include managerial motives, taxes, financial distress, debt over-hang and others.[1] One important implication of these theoretical constructs is that risk management is about the creation and preservation of value rather than the elimination or reduction of risk. Risk is not a bad thing to be eliminated, rather it is a commodity to be created, managed and exchanged.

Some of the results in the literature show how value can be captured by bundling risks appropriately. The risk shifting problem is a classic agency problem that is amenable to risk management solutions. The under-investment problem in its debt over-hang and hidden action and hidden knowledge contexts is also a classic agency problem. The risks imposed by the under-investment problem can be managed in a variety of ways that depend on the source of the problem. Other operating and strategic risks can also be managed.

Jensen and Meckling identified the risk shifting or equivalently asset substitution problem and motivated the rationale for the loss in corporate value. We have seen the construction of and one solution to this problem. The risk shifting problem is a hidden action problem. Bondholders know that management acting in the interests of shareholders can shift value away from the bonds by selecting the riskier investment project once the bonds have been issued. Hence, rationale bondholders require a larger promised payment on the bond instrument. That, *ceteris paribus*, is the source of the agency cost of the debt issue. The cost exists because the firm cannot credibly commit to selecting the safer, more valuable investment project. Green (1984) subsequently showed that the firm could solve the problem by constructing a debt instrument that would provide a credible commitment to the selection of the safer project. The instrument used was a convertible bond contract

---

[1]While the tax motivation for risk management is important, it more than any other has received a significant amount of attention. The results in the literature usually depend on a convex liability function. The after tax earning of the corporation is $\Pi - t(\Pi - \Delta)$ where Δ represents the deductions, e.g., interest on debt, depreciation, etc. If the tax is progressive and the function $t(\cdot)$ is convex then

$$E\{\Pi - t(\Pi - \Delta)\} < E\Pi - t(E\Pi - \Delta)$$

The result is an application of Jensen's Inequality. Since an insurance contract can replace the random earning with the expected earning, it follows that the use of insurance is optimal. While the convex tax function is sufficient, it is not necessary for the result. Suppose that there is a positive probability that the earning will not exceed the deductions and suppose the tax rate is a constant, then the after tax earning becomes $\Pi - t\max\{0, \Pi - \Delta\}$ where $\max\{0, \Pi - \Delta\}$ is convex. Hence

$$E\{\Pi - t\max\{0, \Pi - \Delta\}\} < E\Pi - t\max\{0, E\Pi - \Delta\}$$

This is also an application of Jensen's Inequality and shows that insurance is optimal. While more can be said about the tax motivation for risk management, I will leave it to others.

but the same solution is clearly possible with a bond-warrant package.[2] The action, i.e., selection of the project, was still subsequent to the bond issue but the incentives in the convertible bond were transparent and clearly provided sufficient motivation for management to select the safer project. The agency cost in this case was eliminated with the correct choice of a financing instrument or equivalently an appropriate repackaging of the risks. Hence, the risk shifting problem provides a clear motivation for risk management and will be discussed here in conjunction with the hidden action problem.

Myers identified the under-investment problem due to debt over-hang and the associated loss in corporate value. Subsequently, Myers and Majluf noted hidden knowledge as another motivation for the under-investment problem. In each variant of the problem, management, acting in the interests of shareholders, faces adverse incentives because current shareholders cannot capture the full net present value of the investment project. Myers and Majluf pursued the case of hidden knowledge and showed that if the firm used a new equity issue to finance an investment project, then that hidden knowledge would cause a dilution in the value of the current shareholders stake in the corporation. The dilution would occur because the size of the new issue would have to be large enough to convince outsiders without the hidden knowledge to purchase enough shares to finance the project. Hence the current shareholders would have to yield some of the net present value of the project to the new shareholders; equivalently, the new issue would cause some dilution in the value of the existing shares. A sufficiently large transfer in value would cause the firm to reject a positive net present value project. Two approaches have been pursued to solve the under-investment problem. In the debt over-hang case, Garven and MacMinn showed that by including a bond covenant requiring insurance in the debt instrument, the appropriate incentives could be restored and the under-investment problem eliminated. In the hidden knowledge case, Froot *et al.* showed that an appropriately structured hedge could solve the problem. Hence, the under-investment problem provides a clear motivation for risk management and will be discussed in more detail here in conjunction with the hidden knowledge problem.

As the 1958 Modigliani–Miller Theorem implies the more general result that the value of the corporation is independent of the nexus of contracts

[2]MacMinn also showed that the risk shifting problem could be solved with an appropriately structured insurance contract. See MacMinn, R. D. (1987). "Insurance and Corporate Risk Management." *Journal of Risk and Insurance* 54(4): 658–677. Also see MacMinn, R. D. (1993). "On The Risk Shifting Problem and Convertible Bonds." *Advances in Quantitative Analysis of Finance and Accounting* 2: 181–200, for another explanation and solution method for the risk shifting problem.

that constitute it, we will first turn to a few examples of that proposition. If the generalized theorem were true without qualification, then not only would capital structure be irrelevant but also risk management; neither is irrelevant due in no small part to the *ceteris paribus* conditions in the theorem. The generalization of the theorem does however provide a base case and an indication of where not to look for additional value. In addition, it plays an instrumental role in proving some of the results on the creation of value. This was apparent in the early discussion of the risk shifting problem and its solution. It will be apparent again here in showing a solution to the under-investment problem. Some examples of the generalized 1958 Modigliani–Miller Theorem are considered next. Then we will turn our attention to risk management and the creation of value by considering two crucial problems, i.e., the hidden action and hidden knowledge problems. The solutions to these problems shows that risk management does have value.

A Generalized 1958 Modigliani–Miller Theorem

The earliest results on capital structure theory show that it is irrelevant. The 1958 Modigliani–Miller Theorem showed this irrelevance and provided some direction regarding where to find or where not to find the value in risk management. One popular interpretation of the 1958 Theorem is that no value is created because investors can lever or unlever on their own personal accounts and so will not be willing to pay a premium for a corporation that does the same on corporate account. This interpretation leads to the observation that value can only be created by the corporation if it can provide the investor with an asset or cash flow that cannot be readily duplicated on personal account. Hence, the 1958 Modigliani–Miller Theorem applies to a much wider set of decisions than those the authors may have originally envisioned. The theorem not only makes capital structure irrelevant but it also makes risk management irrelevant, i.e., at least within the *ceteris paribus* conditions of the theorem.

A few examples of a generalized theorem are considered here. The first is concerned with hedging in financial markets.[3] Here we show that the value

[3]Hedging in commodity markets might also be considered. See Holthausen, D (1979). "Hedging and the Competitive Firm Under Price Uncertainty." *American Economic Review* **69**: 989–995, Feder, G. *et al.* (1980). "Futures Market and the Theory of the Firm Under Price Uncertainty." *Quarterly Journal of Economics* **XCIV**: 317–328. These are models of risk averse agents making decisions without recourse to any diversification on personal account and no distinction between personal and corporate account. The corporate form is considered in MacMinn, R. D. (1987). "Forward Markets, Stock Markets, and the Theory of the Firm." *Journal of Finance* **42**(5): 1167–1185, and hedging in commodity markets is shown to have an impact on value through the preservation of tax credits.

of the hedged firm equals that of the unhedged firm. Next, we consider two insurance examples and show that the value of the insured firm equals that of the uninsured firm.

Forward markets

Consider a forward contract. Let Φ denote the unit payoff on a stock index contract and let f denote the forward price. Suppose the unit payoff is increasing in state ξ. The payoff on a forward position is $\varphi(f - \Phi(\xi))$, where φ is the position taken by the firm in futures. Let η be the economic state implicitly defined by the condition $f - \Phi(\eta) = 0$, as shown in Figure 9.1. The payoff on the futures contract is shown in Figure 9.1. The payoff depicted is sometimes referred to as a short position in the futures contract.

The comparison that is instructive is that between the value of the hedged and unhedged corporation. The hedged firm here denotes the firm that takes a position in forward contracts on the stock index fund. The unhedged firm simply has the payoff Π. Suppose the firm is unlevered in the hedged and unhedged cases, so that financial distress does not play a role in the comparison. Let S^u and S^h denote the unhedged and hedged firms respectively. Note that

$$S^u = \int_{\Xi} \Pi(I, \xi)\, dP \tag{9.1}$$

and

$$\begin{aligned} S^h &= \int_{\Xi} \left(\Pi(I, \xi) + \varphi\,(f - \Phi(\xi))\right) dP \\ &= \int_{\Xi} \Pi(I, \xi)\, dP + \varphi \int_{\Xi} (f - \Phi(\xi))\, dP \\ &= S^u \end{aligned} \tag{9.2}$$

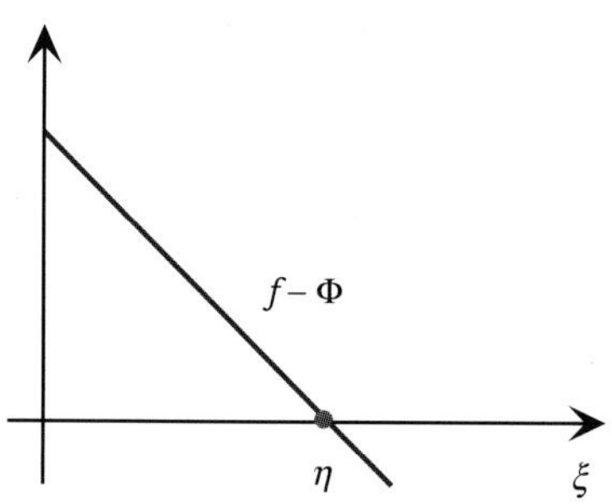

Figure 9.1 Hedging payoff.

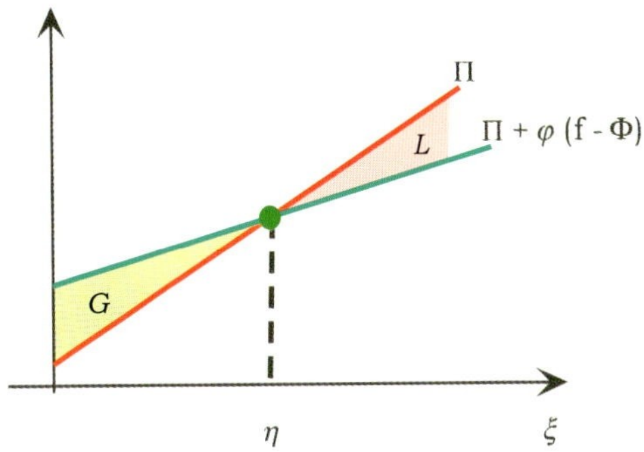

Figure 9.2 Hedged and unhedged corporate payoffs.

The last equality in (9.2) follows because the future value of the forward price must equal the value of the unit stock index payoff *then*, or equivalently, the net present value of the forward on the stock index must be zero in a competitive financial market. Hence, (9.2) yields the result that the value of the hedged firm equals that of the unhedged firm and this is but one corollary to the 1958 Modigliani–Miller Theorem. The hedged and unhedged payoffs for the firm are shown in Figure 9.2. The value of the shaded area represented by G is the gain due to the hedge, while the value of the shaded area represented by L is the loss due to the hedge. Equation (9.2) shows that those values are the same. While no value is added in this unlevered case, it is easy to see that a gain in value is possible if financial distress is possible.

Property insurance contracts

Corporations consist of physical assets that are subject to damage or loss due to accidents or perils; these events generate corporate losses but the events can be insured. Let L denote the random dollar property loss of the corporation and let Π denote the gross payoff of the corporation, i.e., Π does not include the loss. If the firm takes no action to manage the loss then the stock value of the uninsured corporation is S^u where

$$S^u = \int_{\Xi} (\Pi(\xi) - L(\xi))\, dP \tag{9.3}$$

Property insurance contracts typically cover losses above a deductible of d dollars. The payoff on the insurance contract would be $\max\{0, L - d\}$. Note that the property insurance is simply a call option on the loss with an exercise

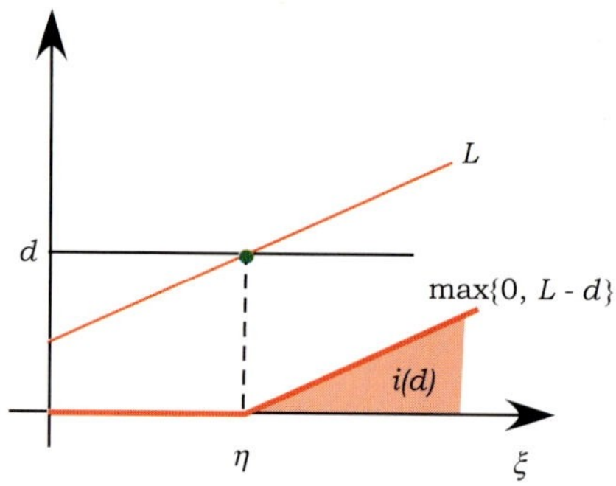

Figure 9.3 Insurance premium.

price equal to the deductible. The premium on the insurance is $i(d)$ where

$$i(d) = \int_{\Xi} \max\{0, L(\xi) - d\}\, dP \tag{9.4}$$

If the firm does insure its property losses then the value of the insured firm is S^i where

$$\begin{aligned} S^i &= -i(d) + \int_{\Xi} \left(\Pi(\xi) - L(\xi) + \max\left\{0, L(\xi) - d\right\}\right) dP \\ &= -i(d) + \int_{\Xi} \max\left\{0, L(\xi) - d\right\} dP + \int_{\Xi} (\Pi(\xi) - L(\xi))\, dP \\ &= S^u \end{aligned} \tag{9.5}$$

The third equality in (9.5) follows because the net present value of the investment in the property insurance is zero. Hence, (9.5) yields the result that the value of the insured firm equals that of the uninsured firm and this is but one more corollary to the 1958 Modigliani–Miller Theorem. The uninsured value is represented in Figure 9.4. The insurance adds to the gross payoff *then* but that addition is equal in value to the insurance premium $i(d)$ paid *now*.

Liability insurance contracts

Corporations consist in part of goods or services that create a liability for the firm. If the firm's goods or services are defective, then the firm may be subject to a liability claim. The product or service liability can be indemnified with insurance. Let L denote the random dollar liability loss of the corporation and let Π denote the gross payoff of the corporation, i.e., Π does not include the loss. If the firm takes no action to manage the loss, then the stock value of the uninsured corporation is S^u given in Equation (9.3).

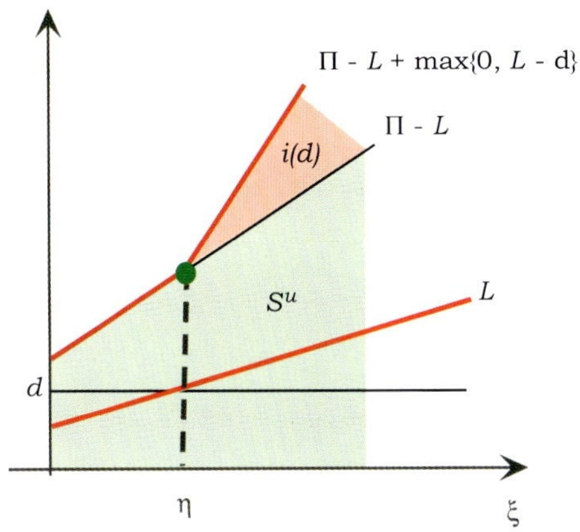

Figure 9.4 Insured and uninsured values with property insurance.

Liability insurance contracts often indemnify the corporation against losses up to some upper limit k. Then the insurance contract payoff is $\min\{L, k\}$ and the insurance premium is $i(k)$ where

$$i(k) = \int_{\Xi} \min\{L, k\}\, dP \tag{9.6}$$

If the firm does insure its property losses, then the value of the insured firm is S^i where

$$\begin{aligned} S^i &= -i(k) + \int_{\Xi} \left(\Pi(\xi) - L(\xi) + \min\{L(\xi), k\}\right) dP \\ &= -i(k) + \int_{\Xi} \min\{L(\xi), k\}\, dP + \int_{\Xi} (\Pi(\xi) - L(\xi))\, dP \\ &= S^u \end{aligned} \tag{9.7}$$

The third equality again follows because the net present value of the investment in insurance is zero. The gross value is shown in Figure 9.5. The additional payoff created *then* just equals the premium paid *now* on the liability policy. Hence, (9.7) yields the result that the value of the insured firm equals that of the uninsured firm and this is but one more corollary to the 1958 Modigliani–Miller Theorem.

Risk Management and Value

Risk management is all about the creation or preservation of value. Incentives can be realigned by restructuring the nexus of risks we call the firm. In

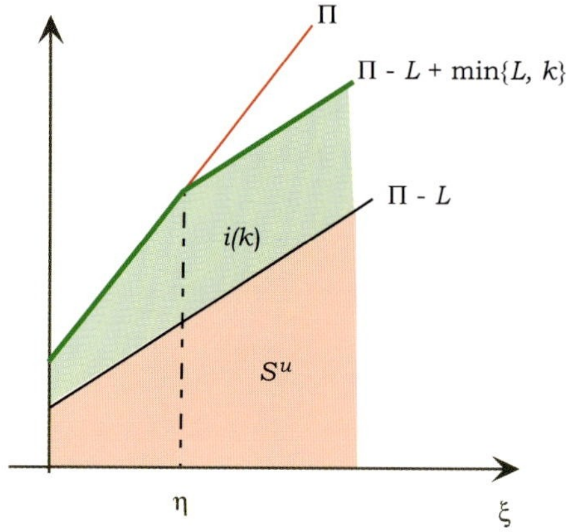

Figure 9.5 Insured and uninsured values with liability insurance.

some cases the incentives become misaligned due to hidden actions. Those incentives can be realigned by bundling contracts to provide credible assurances that the appropriate actions will be taken. In other cases the incentives become misaligned due to hidden knowledge. Even if credible information that reveals what is hidden cannot be given to the market participants, it is still sometimes possible to manage the risks so that optimal decisions that maximize value are still feasible. Equivalently, the agency costs due to hidden knowledge can be avoided if the risks are managed appropriately.

Hidden action

The hidden action problem exists when actions can be taken by management that affect the value of the stakeholders interests in the firm. The hidden action problem can be the source of a variety of problems, including the risk shifting problem and the under-investment problem. Mayers and Smith (1987) described an under-investment problem in the context of an insurance market. There the firm made an investment in capital goods that were subsequently subject to a possible loss in value and the consequent loss in productive capability. The action that was hidden was the firm's choice to take the action to reconstitute the capital goods subsequent to a loss so that the productive capability was maintained. The problem generated an agency cost for the debt issue used to finance the investment. The problem was solved by including a bond covenant requiring sufficient insurance. The bond covenant provided credible assurance that the capital goods would be reconstituted and so the covenant eliminated the agency cost, i.e., see Garven and MacMinn (1993).

Jensen and Meckling described a risk shifting problem. In the classic version of the problem, corporate management finances a capital investment project with a bond issue. The management may choose one of two mutually exclusive investment projects. Both projects require the same capital expenditure but one is riskier than the other in the Rothschild–Stiglitz sense.[4] The ability of management to shift risk to bondholders by switching from a low risk to a high risk investment project creates the problem, e.g., see Jensen and Meckling (1976), Green (1984) and MacMinn (1993).[5] The risk shifting problem has been solved in a variety of ways, e.g., see MacMinn (1987). The ability that management has to shift risk creates the problem and so it can be solved by providing bondholders with a credible assurance that management will not shift the risk. If bonds are issued with a conversion option that yields an option value at least as great as the potential devaluation from risk shifting, then that is a credible assurance and is one way to solve this agency problem.

Hidden knowledge

The hidden knowledge problem occurs when some market agents possess information that is not available to others. From a corporate perspective it yields a necessary distinction between insiders and outsides, or equivalently between those who do and those who do not have the information. For this to be meaningful, of course, the information must by its nature have some value. In this setting as in Chapter 8, it is supposed that the insiders have knowledge about the characteristics of the corporate cash flow; the insiders simply know which of two possible cash flows the corporation has from an investment project. The information has value because it yields the correct net present value for the project.

---

[4]This is the notion that one random project payoff can be described as a mean preserving spread of the other project payoff or equivalently that it has more weight in the tails of its distribution. See Rothschild, M. and J. E. Stiglitz (1970). "Increasing Risk: I. A Definition." *Journal of Economic Theory* 2: 225–243. Also see MacMinn, R. (1981). Lecture Notes on Rothschild and Stiglitz. "Increasing Risk: I. A Definition" at http://macminn.org/uncertainty/risk/rothschild-stiglitz.pdf

[5]There are other examples. The firm must make operating decisions and those decisions are made subsequent to the investment and so the financing decisions. The production decisions are hidden and so a potential source of problems. If the corporate payoff is $\Pi(q, \xi)$ and Π satisfies the principle of increasing uncertainty, i.e., see Leland, H. (1972). "Theory of the Firm Facing Uncertain Demand." *American Economic Review* 62: 278–291, MacMinn, R. D. and A. Holtmann (1983). "Technological Uncertainty and the Theory of the Firm." *Southern Economic Journal* 50: 120–136, then it follows that increasing the production increases risk. It is a simple matter to show that the levered firm has an incentive to produce more than the unlevered firm if the debt is risky.

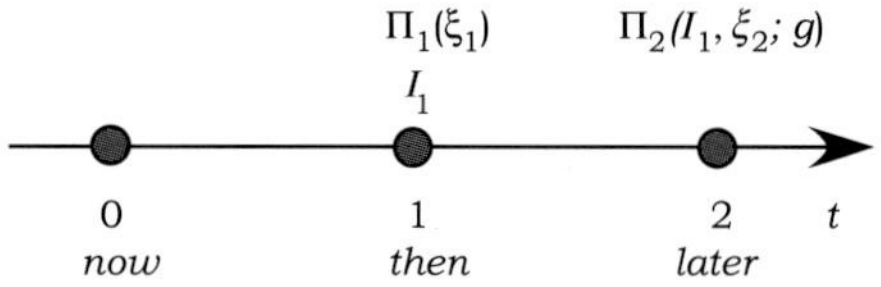

Figure 9.6 Cash flow time line.

Consider a slightly expanded version of the Fisher model here to motivate risk management in the presence of the hidden knowledge problem. Previously, we showed that the corporate manager would make decisions to maximize current shareholder value minus an agency cost; recall that safe debt will be used if possible because it can eliminate the agency cost and allow the optimal investment. Froot *et al.* (1993) noted "... if capital market imperfections make externally obtained funds more expensive than those generated internally, they can generate a rationale for risk management." If the firm has an uncertain cash flow to use in financing its investment and does not manage that risk, then it must either raise cash from external sources if necessary or alter the level of its investment. Either response is simply a reaction to the agency cost. The choice is not actually so stark. The corporate objective function that has been developed shows that the investment will be pushed to the point at which the marginal value of the last dollar invested equals a dollar plus the marginal agency cost. Hence, the firm will raise cash from external sources but the amount will be limited due to the agency cost. The model developed here is motivated by the Froot *et al.* model but the objective function and agency cost are endogenous just as in previous chapters.

Suppose the timeline is extended so that we have dates $t = 0$, 1, and 2 and refer to those dates as *now*, *then* and *later*, respectively. The firm has made decisions in the past, i.e., before *now*, and those decisions have generated an uncertain payoff *then* of Π_1 dollars. In addition, the firm may make an investment decision *then* that yields a payoff of $\Pi_2(I_1, \xi_2; g)$ *later*, if the firm has a good quality investment project and $\Pi_2(I_1, \xi_2; b)$ otherwise where $\Pi_2(I_1, \xi_2; g) > \Pi_2(I_1, \xi_2; b)$ for all ξ_2. The cash flows are summarized in Figure 9.7. The investment *then* is financed with retained earnings, debt or equity. The hidden knowledge problem will apply to the investment payoff *later* but not the payoff Π_1 *then* from previous corporate decisions. The hidden knowledge makes retained earnings, or safe debt preferable to the alternatives. If retained earnings and the safe debt capacity do not suffice, then the risks must be actively managed to allow the firm to avoid the agency cost associated with the hidden knowledge.

Consider the value of the firm *now*. Let Ξ_t denote the set of states of nature *then* and *later*, i.e., for $t = 1$ and 2 respectively. Similarly, let $p_t(\xi_t)$ be the price of a basis stock that pays one dollar in state ξ_t and zero otherwise and let $P_t(\xi_t)$ be the sum of the basis stock prices from zero to ξ_t. Let S_t denote the stock value of the firm at $t = 0, 1, 2$. Then the stock value *now* of the unhedged firm with the good investment opportunity is $S_0^u(I_1; g)$ where

$$S_0^u(I_1; g) = \int_{\Xi_1} \Pi_1^u(\xi_1)\, dP_1 + \int_{\Xi_2} \Pi_2(I_1, \xi_2; g)\, dP_2 \tag{9.8}$$

Of course, the corporate manager does not make the investment decision *now*. Rather she makes that decision *then* when the cash flow $\Pi_1(\xi_1)$ from the corporate operations is known. Assuming that the cash flow is retained, the stock value *then* is $S_1^u(I_1; g)$ where

$$S_1^u(I_1; g) = \Pi_1^u(\xi_1) + \int_{\Xi_2} \Pi_2(I_1, \xi_2; g)\, dP_2 \tag{9.9}$$

The manager of this unhedged corporation with the good investment project makes the investment decision to maximize $S_1^u(I_1; g) - I_1 - c_a(I_1)$ where c_a is the agency cost.[6] Let I_1^* maximize $S_1^u(I_1; g) - I_1$ so that it is the investment that maximizes the net present value or equivalently the current shareholder value. This I_1^* is first best investment but will only be selected if the agency cost is zero. The manager making this investment decision *then* knows the corporate earnings $\Pi_1^u(\xi_1)$ and the manager knows how much safe debt can be issued in the presence of the hidden knowledge problem. Given rationale expectations about the size of the investments made by firms with good and bad projects, the maximum promised payment that the manager can make and avoid any agency cost due to the hidden knowledge is the dollar promise $b_2^* = \Pi_2(I_1, 0; b)$[7] as shown in Figure 9.7. Let $D_1(b_2^*)$ be the value of the debt issue where

$$D_1(b_2^*) = \int_{\Xi_2} b_2^*\, dP_2 \tag{9.10}$$

Now it is apparent that the manager of the firm with the good investment project can avoid the agency cost of the hidden knowledge problem if the corporate earnings *now* and the safe debt capacity suffice to raise the optimal investment expenditure. Equivalently, the agency cost can be eliminated if $\Pi_1^u(\xi_1) + D_1(b_2^*) > I_1^*$. Without further action, there is no guarantee that this inequality will be satisfied *then*.

[6] See Chapter 8 for the derivation of this objective function.

[7] Of course, if $\Pi_2(I_1, 0; b) = 0$ then there is no feasible safe debt issue.

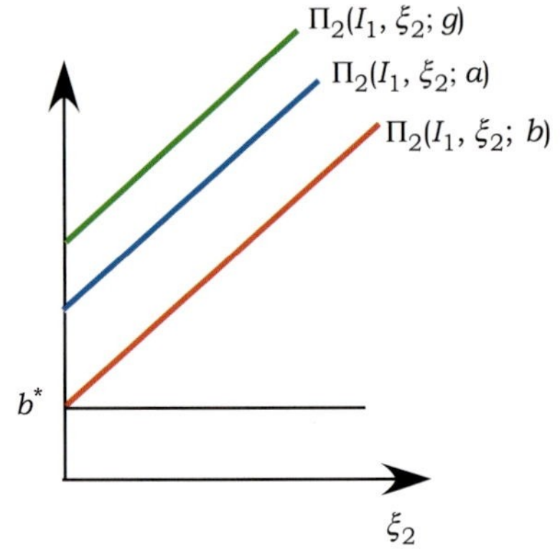

Figure 9.7 Safe debt capacity given hidden knowledge.

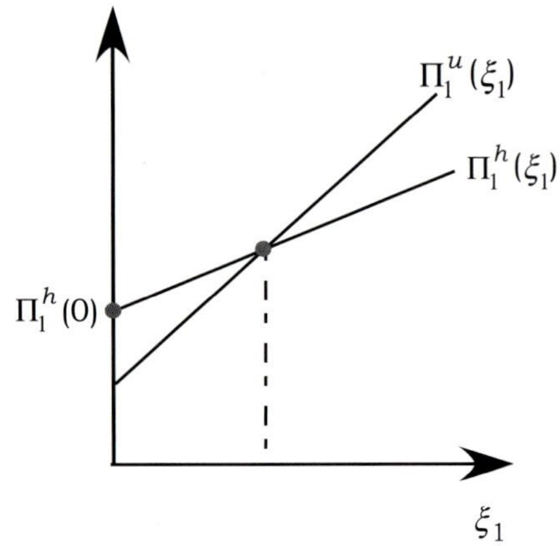

Figure 9.8 Hedging to manage the risk of earnings *then*.

Consider the manager making decisions *now*. The manager is not due to make a decision about the size of the investment in the capital project until *then*, but the manager can make decisions *now* to manage the risk of having enough money *then* to make the optimal investment choice. Without any risk management decisions *now*, the firm may or may not have enough cash flow *then* from corporate operations to finance the optimal investment with retained earnings and safe debt. Hence, in the absence of risk management, the firm may have to raise additional money externally with a risky bond issue or an equity issue. In either case, the associated agency cost will cause an under-investment problem and value will be lost. With risk management decisions *now*, it is possible to eliminate or at least alleviate the agency costs due to the hidden knowledge problem.

Consider risk management decisions that can be made *now* that will circumvent the under-investment problem. Suppose the manager hedges the corporate earnings *then* by purchasing a forward contract. Also suppose that safe debt can be issued on the investment project undertaken *then* and let b_2^* be the maximum promised payment consistent with a transparent valuation of the debt issue by outsiders. The forward contract will yield a corporate payoff *then* of $\Pi_1^h(\xi_1) = \Pi_1^u(\xi_1) + \varphi(f_1 - \Phi(\xi_1))$ and the debt issue will yield a cash flow *then* of $D_1(b_2^*)$. If the hedge can be designed so that $\Pi_1^h(\xi_1) \geq I_1^* - D_1(b_2^*)$ for all ξ_1, then these risk management and financing decisions combine to eliminate the under-investment problem. If the corporate payoff *then* is increasing across states, then the under-investment problem can be eliminated by creating a hedge sufficient to make $\Pi_1^h(0) \geq I_1^* - D_1(b_2^*)$, i.e., see Figure 9.8.

$$
\begin{aligned}
S_0^h(I_1^*; g) &= \int_{\Xi_1} \Pi_1^h(\xi_1)\, dP_1 + \int_{\Xi_2} \Pi_2(I_1^*, \xi_2; g)\, dP_2 \\
&= \int_{\Xi_1} \Pi_1^u(\xi_1)\, dP_1 + \varphi \int_{\Xi_1} \big(f_1 - \Phi(\xi_1)\big)\, dP_1 + \int_{\Xi_2} \Pi_2(I_1^*, \xi_2; g)\, dP_2 \\
&= \int_{\Xi_1} \Pi_1^u(\xi_1)\, dP_1 + \int_{\Xi_2} \Pi_2(I_1^*, \xi_2; g)\, dP_2 \qquad (9.11) \\
&= \int_{\Xi_1} \Pi_1^u(\xi_1)\, dP_1 + \int_{\Xi_2} \Pi_2(I_1^a, \xi_2; g)\, dP_2 \\
&\quad + \left(\int_{\Xi_2} \Pi_2(I_1^*, \xi_2; g)\, dP_2 - \int_{\Xi_2} \Pi_2(I_1^a, \xi_2; g)\, dP_2 \right) \\
&= S_0^u(I_1^a; g) + c_a(I_1^a)
\end{aligned}
$$

The second equality in (9.11) follows because the net present value of the forward position is zero. This is due to the corollary of the 1958 Modigliani–Miller Theorem and becomes quite useful here because the cost of hedging is zero but unlike the corollary, there is value to be gained here by managing the risk of having enough retained earnings available for investment *then*. Hence, the firm can increase value through appropriate risk management decisions designed to eliminate the agency cost associated with the hidden knowledge problem. Equation (9.11) shows that risk management can recapture the entire agency cost.

Caviar Caveat

Hedging can sometimes increase risk and so risk management notions must be used carefully and in some cases avoided because they increase rather than decrease risk. In the extreme case of Russian caviar, the intuition is that the product price tracks the random exchange rate E and so hedging would increase rather than decrease risk. Suppose that a firm sells caviar in this country and $P(\xi)$ is the random domestic product price *then*. Suppose q represents the number of units sold *then*, r represents the price in rubles and $E(\xi)$ is the inverse of the currency exchange rate, i.e., dollars per ruble. The firm payoff then is $\Pi(\xi) = P(\xi)q - E(\xi)rq$. If the price is determined competitively *then*, it follows that the price must be $P(\xi) = E(\xi)r + c$ for each state ξ, where c is a unit cost of carry. In this case, it is quite apparent that the product price and the reciprocal of the currency exchange rate are perfectly positively correlated.

Let $\Pi^u = Pq - Erq$ denote the payoff of the unhedged firm. Suppose the firm buys rubles forward to pay for its caviar purchases. Let f denote the forward exchange rate. Then the hedged payoff is $\Pi^h = Pq - Erq_s - frq_f$, where $q = q_s + q_f$. The hedged payoff may also be expressed as

$$\begin{aligned} \Pi^h &= Pq - \mathrm{E}rq - (f - \mathrm{E})\, rq_f \\ &= \Pi^u - (f - \mathrm{E})\, rq_f \end{aligned} \tag{9.12}$$

Observe first that the unhedged payoff is cq and second that the hedged payoff increases or decreases as the spot exchange rate is greater or less than the forward rate, i.e.,

$$\begin{aligned} \frac{\partial \Pi^h}{\partial q_f} &= c - (f - E(\xi))\, r \\ &\gtrless c \quad \text{as } E(\xi) \gtrless f \end{aligned} \tag{9.13}$$

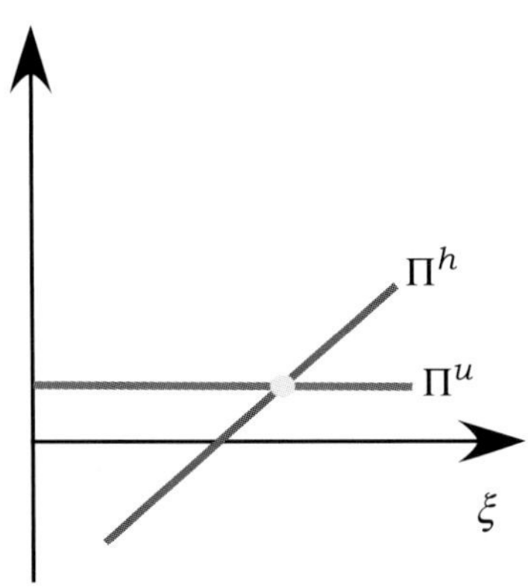

Figure 9.9 Hedged versus unhedged payoffs.

and so the hedged payoff rotates counter clockwise through the forward rate as the hedge increases. This, however, increases rather than decreases the risk of the payoff and provides one strikingly simple example of when a hedge is really speculation.

Suggested Problems

1. A generalization of 1958 Modigliani–Miller Theorem suggests that if firms r and t merge so that the payoff of the merged firm is the sum of the payoffs of the unmerged firms, then the stock value of the merged firm equals the sum of the values of the unmerged firms. Demonstrate this claim.
2. Suppose the corporation described in the section on hidden knowledge faces random liability losses of L dollars *then*. Will an insurance purchase be an effective management technique in solving the under-investment problem described there?
3. Consider the corporation described in the section on hidden knowledge. Suppose the corporation has random earnings *then* from its operations in the domestic and foreign markets and has investment opportunities in both markets *then* as well. Should the firm hedge the currency risks *now*? What other risk management techniques might increase corporate value? If the firm levers its capital investments, then where should it do the borrowing?

Chapter 10

Concluding Remarks

The Fisher model provides the foundation for more than a demonstration of the origins of the net present value rule under certainty. The received theory of corporate finance can be posited in the context of the Fisher model under uncertainty as the analysis here has shown. The separation theorems in Chapters 4 and 8 are particularly important because they provide the basis for an endogenous determination of the corporate objective function. The objective function does not need to be and in fact should not be assumed as it so often has been in the literature.

The modeling also provides a framework for stating and proving the classic theorems in corporate finance some of which were demonstrated in Chapter 6. In the subsequent chapters the hidden action and hidden knowledge problems were exposited. The hidden action problem arises when corporate management can make decisions and take actions that affect the value of corporate assets unknown to the stakeholders who value those assets in the financial markets. The hidden action problem is the source of a variety of agency problems in corporate finance. The risk shift problem arises due to a hidden action and can be solved by reconstructing the risks that constitute the corporation as was demonstrated in Chapter 7. The under-investment problem can arise in a variety of ways and the hidden action problem is one cause of the problem as was demonstrated in Chapter 7 also. The hidden knowledge problem arises when corporate management possesses information that investors do not. This information is valuable but difficult at best to convey to investors or equivalently corporate outsiders. Hidden knowledge is also the source of agency problems in corporate finance and the most well-known consequence of hidden knowledge is an under-investment problem.

Even though the hidden knowledge problem complicates the analysis because corporate insiders cannot trade on the basis of insider information, a separation result was still demonstrated in Chapter 8 in the process of demonstrating the Myers–Majluf pecking order theorem.

The Fisher model also provides a natural place to begin a study of corporate risk management. Most of the theorems in corporate finance are concerned with capital structure or dividend policy but these concepts are concerned with packaging or repackaging risks and can be viewed as special cases of risk management. Some risk management notions are introduced in Chapter 9. The risk shifting problem and an under-investment problem both due to hidden actions are reconsidered in Chapter 9; risk management solutions to these problems exist and are discussed. The hidden knowledge problem and the consequent under-investment problem is also discussed and a risk management solution provided by Froot *et al.* is reframed and demonstrated in the Fisher setting.

The Fisher model provides the framework and basis for generating all of the important theorems in corporate finance. Some of the classic theorems have been demonstrated here but far more is possible. The model is sufficiently malleable for generalizations and theorems not yet stated.

Bibliography

Alchian, A. A. and H. Demsetz (1972). "Production, Information Costs, and Economic Organization." *American Economic Review* **62**(5): 777–795.

Allen, F. and G. R. Faulhaber (1989). "Signaling by Underpricing in the IPO Market." *Journal of Financial Economics* **23**(2): 303–323.

Arrow, K. J. (1963). "The Role of Securities in the Optimal Allocation of Risk Bearing." *Review of Economic Studies* **31**(2): 91–96.

Arrow, K. J. (1984). "The Theory of Risk Aversion." *Collected Papers of Kenneth J. Arrow* **3**: 147–171. Harvard University Press.

Baron, D. P. (1976). "Default Risk and the Modigliani–Miller Theorem: A Synthesis." *American Economic Review* **66**(1): 204–212.

Bhattacharya, S. (1980). "Nondissipative Signaling Structures and Dividend Policy." *Quarterly Journal of Economics* **95**(1): 1–24.

Bodie, Z. and R. Taggart (1978). "Future Investment Opportunities and the Value of the Call Provision on a Bond." *Journal of Finance* **33**: 1187–1200.

Brennan, M. and A. Kraus (1987). "Efficient Financing under Asymmetric Information." *Journal of Finance* **XLII**(5): 1225–1243.

DeAngelo, H. and R. Masulis (1980). "Optimal Capital Structure Under Corporate and Personal Taxation." *Journal of Financial Economics* **8**: 3–29.

Debreu, G. (1959). *Theory of Value: An Axiomatic Analysis of Economic Equilibrium.* John Wiley & Sons.

Diamond, P. (1967). "The Role of a Stock Market in a General Equilibrium Model with Technological Uncertainty." *American Economic Review* **57**: 759–773.

Ekern, S. and R. Wilson (1974). "On the Theory of the Firm in an Economy with Incomplete Markets." *Bell Journal of Economics* **5**: 171–180.

Feder, G. *et al.* (1980). "Futures Market and the Theory of the Firm Under Price Uncertainty." *Quarterly Journal of Economics* **XCIV**: 317–328.

Fisher, I. (1930). *The Theory of Interest.* New York, MacMillan.

Froot, K. A. *et al.* (1993). "Risk Management: Coordinating Corporate Investment and Financing Policies." *Journal of Finance* **48**(5): 1629–1658.

Froot, K. A. *et al.* (1994). "A Framework for Risk Management." *Harvard Business Review* **Nov–Dec**: 91–102.

Garman, M. (1979). A Synthesis of the Pure Theory of Arbitrage. Working Paper No. 98, Institute of Business and Economic Research, University of California at Berkeley.

Garven, J. R. and R. D. MacMinn (1993). "The Underinvestment Problem, Bond Covenants and Insurance." *Journal of Risk and Insurance* **60**(4): 635–646.

Glazer, J. and R. Israel (1990). "Managerial Incentives and Financial Signaling in Product Market Competition." *International Journal of Industrial Organization* **8**(2): 271–280.

Green, R. C. (1984). "Investment Incentives, Debt and Warrants." *Journal of Financial Economics* **13**: 115–136.

Hirshleifer, J. (1965). "Investment Decision Under Uncertainty: Choice-Theoretic Approaches." *Quarterly Journal of Economics* **79**(4): 509–536.

Holthausen, D. (1979). "Hedging and the Competitive Firm Under Price Uncertainty." *American Economic Review* **69**: 989–995.

Jensen, M. and W. Meckling (1976). "Theory of the Firm: Managerial Behavior, Agency Costs and Ownership Structure." *Journal of Financial Economics* **3**: 305–360.

Jensen, M. and C. Smith (1985). "Stockholder, Manager, and Creditor Interests: Applications of Agency Theory." *Recent Advances in Corporate Finance*. E. Altman and M. Subrahmanyam, eds. Richard D. Irwin.

Kimball, M. S. (1990). "Precautionary Saving in the Small and in the Large." *Econometrica* **58**: 53–73.

Kohn, M. (1999). Risk Instruments in the Medieval and Early Modern Economy. Working Paper 99-07, Dartmouth College.

Leland, H. (1972). "Theory of the Firm Facing Uncertain Demand." *American Economic Review* **62**: 278–291.

Leland, H. and D. Pyle (1977). "Informational Asymmetries, Financial Structure and Financial Intermediation." *Journal of Finance* **32**: 371–387.

MacMinn, R. (1980). Lecture Notes on Arrow's "The Theory of Risk Aversion".

MacMinn, R. (1981). Lecture Notes on Rothschild and Stiglitz's "Increasing Risk: I. A Definition".

MacMinn, R. (1984). Lecture Notes on Pratt's "Risk Aversion in the Small and in the Large".

MacMinn, R. (1987). "Lecture Notes on the Risk-Shifting Problem."

MacMinn, R. (1995). Lecture Notes on Ekern and Wilson's "On the Theory of the Firm in an Economy with Incomplete Markets".

MacMinn, R. D. (1987). "Forward Markets, Stock Markets, and the Theory of the Firm." *Journal of Finance* **42**(5): 1167–1185.

MacMinn, R. D. (1987). "Insurance and Corporate Risk Management." *Journal of Risk and Insurance* **54**(4): 658–677.

MacMinn, R. D. (1993). "On the Risk Shifting Problem and Convertible Bonds." *Advances in Quantitative Analysis of Finance and Accounting* **2**: 181–200.

MacMinn, R. D. and A. Holtmann (1983). "Technological Uncertainty and the Theory of the Firm." *Southern Economic Journal* **50**: 120–136.

MacMinn, R. and J. Martin (1988). "Uncertainty, the Fisher Model, and Corporate Financial Theory." *Research in Finance* 7. Greenwich, Connecticut, JAI Press Inc.

MacMinn, R. and F. Page (1995). "Stock Options, Managerial Incentives, and Capital Structure." *Journal of Financial Studies* Dec.

Main, B. G. (1983). "Corporate Insurance Purchases and Taxes." *Journal of Risk and Insurance* 197–223.

Markowitz, H. M. (1952). "Portfolio Selection." *Journal of Finance* 7(1): 77–91.

Mayers, D. and C. Smith (1982). "On the Corporate Demand for Insurance." *Journal of Business* 55: 281–296.

Mayers, D. and C. W. J. Smith (1987). "Corporate Insurance and the Underinvestment Problem." *Journal of Risk and Insurance* 45–54.

McNichols, M. and A. Dravid (1990). "Stock Dividends, Stock Splits, and Signaling." *Journal of Finance* **45**(3): 857–879.

Miller, M. and F. Modigliani (1961). "Dividend Policy, Growth, and the Valuation of Shares." *Journal of Business* **34**(4): 411–433.

Miller, M. H. (1977). "Debt and Taxes." *Journal of Finance* **32**(2): 261–275.

Modigliani, F. and M. H. Miller (1958). "The Cost of Capital, Corporation Finance and the Theory of Investment." *American Economic Review* **48**(2): 261–297.

Mossin, J. (1966). "Equilibrium in a Capital Asset Market." *Econometrica* **34**: 768–783.

Myers, S. C. (1977). "The Determinants of Corporate Borrowing." *Journal of Financial Economics* **5**: 147–175.

Myers, S. C. and N. S. Majluf (1984). "Corporate Financing and Investment Decisions When Firms Have Information That Investors Do Not Have." *Journal of Financial Economics* **13**: 187–221.

Noe, T. (1988). "Capital Structure and Signaling Game Equilibria." *Review of Financial Studies* **1**: 331–356.

Pratt, J. W. (1964). "Risk Aversion in the Small and in the Large." *Econometrica* **32**: 122–136.

Radner, R. (1974). "A Note on Unanimity of Stockholder's Preferences Among Alternative Production Plans: A Reformulation of the Ekern-Wilson Model." *Bell Journal of Economics* **5**: 181–184.

Riley, J. G. (1985). "Competition with Hidden Knowledge." *Journal of Political Economy* **93**(5): 958–976.

Rothschild, M. and J. E. Stiglitz (1970). "Increasing Risk: I. A Definition." *Journal of Economic Theory* **2**: 225–243.

Sandmo, A. (1970). "The Effect of Uncertainty on Saving Decisions." *Review of Economic Studies* **37**: 353–360.

Sharpe, W. F. (1964). "Capital Asset Prices: A Theory of Market Equilibrium Under Conditions of Risk." *Journal of Finance* **19**(3): 425–442.

Smith, C. and J. Warner (1979). "On Financial Contracting: An Analysis of Bond Covenants." *Journal of Financial Economics* **7**: 117–161.

Smith, C. W. and R. M. Stulz (1985). "The Determinants of Firms' Hedging Policies." *Journal of Financial and Quantitative Analysis* **20**(4): 391–405.

Sobel, J. *et al.* (1990). "Fixed-Equilibrium Rationalizability in Signaling Games." *Journal of Economic Theory* **52**(2): 304–331.

Stiglitz, J. E. (1969). "A Re-Examination of the Modigliani–Miller Theorem." *American Economic Review* **59**(5): 78–93.

Stulz, R. M. (1984). "Optimal Hedging Policies." *Journal of Financial and Quantitative Analysis* **19**(2): 127–140.

Index